The World's Oldest Stories: Mythology from Around the Globe

Anam Rasheed

Published by Anam Rasheed, 2024.

While every precaution has been taken in the preparation of this book, the publisher assumes no responsibility for errors or omissions, or for damages resulting from the use of the information contained herein.

THE WORLD'S OLDEST STORIES: MYTHOLOGY FROM AROUND THE GLOBE

First edition. October 9, 2024.

Copyright © 2024 Anam Rasheed.

ISBN: 979-8227572196

Written by Anam Rasheed.

Table of Contents

Prologue 1
Chapter 1: The Trickster Tales of Anansi 2
Chapter 2: Amaterasu and the Japanese Sun 6
Chapter 3: The Magic of Norse Yggdrasil 10
Chapter 4: The Heroic Adventures of Gilgamesh 15
Chapter 5: The Egyptian God Ra's Journey 20
Chapter 6: The Tale of Maui and the Sun 25
Chapter 7: The Thunder of Zeus and the Olympians 29
Chapter 8: The Dreamtime of the Aboriginal Ancestors 34
Chapter 9: The Mysterious Phoenix of Ancient China 39
Chapter 10: The Underworld Voyage of Izanagi 44
Chapter 11: The Coyote's Clever Tricks in American Lore 49
Chapter 12: The Legend of Ganesha and His Elephant Head 54
Chapter 13: The Aztec Creation Story of the Fifth Sun 59
Chapter 14: The Guardians of the Inca Andes 64
Chapter 15: The Celtic Story of the Salmon of Wisdom 68
Chapter 16: The Love Story of Odin and Frigg 73
Chapter 17: The Mystical Journey of the Rainbow Serpent 78
Chapter 18: The Russian Baba Yaga and Her Magical Hut 82
Chapter 19: The Mayan Twins' Underworld Challenge 86
Chapter 20: The Dragon and the Pearl 90
Epilogue 95

Prologue

Long, long ago, before the days of science and technology, people looked up at the sky, into the forests, across vast oceans, and wondered about the mysteries of the world. Why does the sun rise every morning? Why does thunder roar? What happens after we leave this world? To answer these big questions, our ancestors created stories—fantastic tales of brave heroes, tricky gods, magical creatures, and mysterious lands.

These stories were more than just entertainment; they were ways to explain the unexplainable, teach important lessons, and bring people together around a campfire or under a starry sky. Some stories were filled with adventure, while others spoke of love, loss, or the beginning of everything we know. These myths, passed down from generation to generation, have shaped cultures and communities for thousands of years. They've traveled across mountains, crossed seas, and even been whispered among the winds of time.

In this book, we are about to take a journey back to those ancient days. We'll explore the tales that people from all corners of the earth told—the myths that still spark wonder and curiosity today. From the snowy peaks of Norse mythology to the warm sands of Egyptian legends, from the deep forests of the Amazon to the temples of Japan, every story in this book will bring you closer to understanding how people made sense of the wonders and challenges of the world around them.

So, settle in, and let your imagination soar as we step into these timeless tales, full of tricksters, gods, monsters, and heroes. The stories you are about to read are among the world's oldest and most cherished—woven from dreams, fears, hopes, and the magic of human creativity. Welcome to a journey around the globe through the myths that helped shape humanity itself.

Chapter 1: The Trickster Tales of Anansi

Anansi, the trickster spider, is one of the most famous characters in African mythology, especially from the Ashanti people of Ghana. He's a tiny spider, but don't let his size fool you—Anansi is clever, mischievous, and always trying to outsmart everyone around him. His tales have been passed down through generations, spreading to different parts of the world, especially through the Caribbean, where his stories became even more well-known. Though he's not the strongest or the fastest, Anansi uses his brain to get what he wants, and sometimes, he teaches important lessons along the way.

Anansi is often shown as a spider, but in some stories, he can take on human form or a mix of both. Imagine a creature with the body of a spider but the face and voice of a person! His name means "spider" in the Ashanti language, but his clever tricks and funny adventures are what make him memorable.

One of the most famous stories about Anansi is how he became the "owner of all stories." A long time ago, all the stories in the world belonged to Nyame, the Sky God. Nyame kept the stories in the sky, far away from anyone else. Anansi, who wanted to own the stories himself, decided to go to Nyame and ask for them. But, of course, Nyame wouldn't just give the stories away. He told Anansi that he could only have the stories if he could capture three powerful and dangerous creatures: the python, the leopard, and the hornets. These animals were no easy catch, but Anansi, being the trickster he was, thought up a clever plan.

First, Anansi set out to capture the python. Instead of using strength, Anansi tricked the python into tying itself up! He told the python that he had heard someone say the python was not as long as a nearby stick. The python, eager to prove Anansi wrong, agreed to lie down next to the stick to compare. As the python stretched out, Anansi quickly tied it up, just as he had planned.

Next, Anansi needed to capture the leopard, a fierce and dangerous animal. But Anansi wasn't scared. He dug a deep hole and covered it with leaves, then waited. The leopard, not seeing the trap, fell right into the hole. When the leopard cried for help, Anansi pretended to offer assistance. Instead, he tricked the leopard into tying itself up so that Anansi could "pull it out of the hole," but really, Anansi was just capturing it.

Finally, Anansi needed to deal with the hornets. He knew he couldn't fight them because hornets are small but mighty. Instead, Anansi filled a gourd with water and sprinkled it around the hornets' nest. He told the hornets that it was raining and that they should hide in his gourd to stay dry. Believing Anansi, the hornets all flew into the gourd, and Anansi quickly sealed it shut.

With all three challenges complete, Anansi returned to Nyame, the Sky God. Impressed by Anansi's cleverness, Nyame kept his promise and gave Anansi the ownership of all stories. From that day on, Anansi became the "King of Stories," and people around the world began telling his tales.

Anansi's stories aren't just about him being sneaky or mischievous; they often carry important lessons. For example, in some stories, Anansi's tricks backfire, and he ends up in trouble himself. These stories teach that while it's good to be clever, being greedy or dishonest can sometimes lead to problems. Other stories show how Anansi, though small and weak compared to bigger animals, uses his intelligence to overcome obstacles. This teaches the lesson that brains can often be more powerful than brawn, and that thinking carefully about a situation can help you find a solution that others might not see.

One story that shows this is the tale of "Anansi and the Pot of Wisdom." In this story, Nyame, the Sky God, once again plays a part. He had a pot that held all the wisdom in the world, and Anansi wanted it for himself. Nyame agreed to give Anansi the pot, but he didn't tell him how to use it. Anansi, thinking he should keep all the wisdom for himself, decided to hide the pot up in a tree. He tied the pot around his neck and started to climb. But because the pot was heavy and awkward, Anansi struggled to get up the tree. His son, who had been watching him, called out, "Why don't you tie the pot to your back instead? It will be easier that way." Anansi, embarrassed that he hadn't thought of such a simple solution, realized that even though he had all the wisdom in the world, he didn't know everything. In frustration, he dropped the pot, and it broke into pieces, spreading wisdom all over the world for everyone to share.

This story shows that even the cleverest person can still learn from others, and that wisdom isn't something that one person should keep to themselves. It's something that should be shared with everyone, so that the world can become a better place.

Anansi's trickster nature also shows up in his interactions with other animals. In many stories, he's always trying to get the best of his friends, like Turtle or Rabbit, by playing tricks on them. In one story, Anansi invites Turtle to a feast but plays a mean trick. When Turtle arrives, Anansi tells him he must wash his hands before eating. Turtle, being a slow creature, goes to the river to wash, but by the time he returns, Anansi has eaten all the food! Turtle, however, gets his revenge by inviting Anansi to a feast at the river, where Anansi struggles because he can't swim. This back-and-forth between the characters shows how sometimes, tricking others can lead to getting tricked yourself.

Anansi's stories also traveled far and wide. When people from Africa were taken to the Caribbean and the Americas during the transatlantic slave trade, they brought their stories with them. Anansi's tales blended with local folklore and became popular in places like Jamaica, where he's often known as "Brer Anansi." These stories helped people remember their culture and brought a sense of hope, especially in tough times. Anansi, with his quick thinking and cleverness, became a symbol of resilience and survival.

Though he's sometimes sneaky and a little selfish, Anansi's stories have entertained people for centuries, and they continue to be told today. His clever tricks, funny adventures, and the lessons he teaches make him one of the most memorable characters in mythology. Whether he's outsmarting a leopard, tricking a snake, or learning an important lesson about sharing wisdom, Anansi shows us that being clever is about using your mind, but it's also about knowing when to be kind and when to let others win.

Chapter 2: Amaterasu and the Japanese Sun

Amaterasu is one of the most important figures in Japanese mythology. She is the goddess of the sun and the ruler of the heavens, known for her bright and radiant light. Her name, "Amaterasu," means "shining in heaven," and she is considered the source of all life because the sun's light is necessary for things to grow. In the old stories told by the Japanese, she plays a crucial role in keeping balance and harmony in the world. But her story isn't just about the sun shining peacefully in the sky—there are many adventures and challenges that Amaterasu faces, and her legend is filled with drama, lessons, and a deep connection to nature.

Amaterasu was born from the left eye of the god Izanagi, who, along with his sister-wife Izanami, created the islands of Japan. After Izanami passed away, Izanagi was devastated and went on a journey to the underworld to try and bring her back, but things didn't go as planned. When he returned from this dark and frightening place, he performed a cleansing ritual, and during this ritual, Amaterasu was born, shining brilliantly from his eye. Her siblings, Tsukuyomi, the god of the moon, and Susanoo, the god of storms and seas, were also born during this ritual, but it was clear that Amaterasu was the most powerful. Izanagi was so impressed by her brightness that he gave her the responsibility of ruling the heavens and lighting up the world.

Amaterasu was a kind and just ruler, making sure that the sun rose every day to nourish the Earth and help crops grow, but her relationship with her brother Susanoo wasn't always peaceful. Susanoo was wild and chaotic, and he didn't like following rules. He often caused trouble, and although Amaterasu tried to be patient with him, there was one event that pushed her too far. Susanoo, in one of his fits of anger, stormed through Amaterasu's fields, ruining all the crops she had worked so hard to grow. He even destroyed her sacred rice paddies, which were a symbol of the people's survival and well-being. This wasn't just about crops being lost—rice was the main food of the Japanese people, and it was believed to be a gift from the gods. By destroying the rice fields, Susanoo was not only harming Amaterasu's work but also the people who depended on the food.

But the worst thing that Susanoo did was far more personal. In a moment of rage, Susanoo threw a flayed horse (a sacred animal in Japanese culture) into Amaterasu's weaving hall, where she and her maidens were creating beautiful garments for the gods. The shock and horror of this act were too much for Amaterasu to bear. She was deeply hurt, not just because of the destruction but because of the lack of respect her brother showed her. In her grief and anger, Amaterasu decided to hide herself away. She retreated to a cave, called the "Heavenly Rock Cave," and blocked the entrance with a large stone. With Amaterasu hidden inside the cave, the world was plunged into darkness.

Without the sun, everything began to fall apart. Crops withered, and the people grew desperate. Darkness spread across the land, and even the other gods became worried. They realized that without Amaterasu's light, life couldn't survive. They needed to figure out a way to bring her out of the cave, but Amaterasu was so upset that she refused to leave. The gods held a council and discussed various ways to lure her out, but nothing seemed to work. It was then that one of the gods, Uzume, came up with a clever plan.

Uzume was the goddess of joy and laughter, and she decided to use her talents to cheer everyone up and, hopefully, coax Amaterasu out of hiding. She gathered the other gods outside the cave and began dancing in the most outrageous, funny way. She put on a silly performance, stomping her feet, shaking her body, and even performing a comical striptease! The other gods couldn't help but laugh at Uzume's ridiculous antics, and soon, their laughter filled the air.

Amaterasu, who was still inside the cave, could hear all the noise. She became curious. How could there be so much laughter and joy when the world was supposed to be in darkness? Peeking out from behind the stone blocking the cave, Amaterasu asked what was going on. One of the gods told her that they were celebrating because they had found a new, brighter goddess to take her place. Intrigued and a little jealous, Amaterasu stepped out of the cave to see what was happening. As soon as she did, the gods quickly moved the stone, blocking her from retreating back inside.

At that moment, the world was flooded with light again. The sun returned, and life began to flourish once more. The crops could grow, and balance was restored to the heavens and Earth. The gods begged Amaterasu to never hide again, reminding her of how important her light was to the world. She agreed but only after Susanoo was punished for his behavior. Susanoo was banished from the heavens, forced to wander the Earth, and learn from his mistakes. Amaterasu resumed her place in the sky, continuing to shine her light on the world, ensuring that life could thrive.

This story about Amaterasu isn't just about a goddess of the sun—it's about the balance between light and dark, order and chaos. It shows how important harmony is in the world and how even gods can feel pain, frustration, and sadness. Amaterasu's retreat into the cave symbolizes the times when things go wrong, and we feel like hiding from the world. But just like in the story, there's always a way to bring light back. The laughter of Uzume and the support of the other gods show how community and joy can heal even the deepest wounds.

Amaterasu is also seen as the ancestor of Japan's emperors. According to legend, her grandson, Ninigi, was sent down from the heavens to rule over the Earth, bringing with him three sacred treasures: a mirror, a jewel, and a sword. These treasures are still a part of Japanese imperial tradition, symbolizing wisdom, benevolence, and valor. The mirror, especially, is significant because it represents

Amaterasu herself. In fact, the mirror used to lure her out of the cave is said to have become a sacred object, showing her reflection and reminding her of her beauty and power.

Amaterasu's influence extends far beyond just being the goddess of the sun. In Japanese culture, she represents life, warmth, and the cycles of nature. Her story teaches people about the importance of light, not just the physical light of the sun, but the light that exists in everyone—the inner light of kindness, joy, and strength. Even when things get dark, Amaterasu reminds us that there's always a way to bring brightness back into our lives.

Amaterasu continues to be celebrated in Japan today, especially at the Ise Grand Shrine, which is dedicated to her. Every year, people visit the shrine to honor her and give thanks for the sun's life-giving power. The shrine is one of the most important religious sites in Japan, and the rituals performed there connect modern-day people to the ancient traditions and stories of their ancestors.

Through her story, Amaterasu reminds us of the power of light, the importance of balance, and the value of community. She shows that even when faced with great sadness or anger, the light can return, bringing hope, growth, and harmony to the world once more. Her legend is a beautiful reminder that, just like the sun, we all have the power to shine brightly, even after dark times.

Chapter 3: The Magic of Norse Yggdrasil

Yggdrasil, in Norse mythology, is often called the "World Tree" and plays an incredibly important role in the stories of the ancient Norse people. Imagine a gigantic, towering tree with branches that stretch out over the entire universe and roots that dig deep into the different realms of existence. It's not just any ordinary tree—Yggdrasil is magical and holds everything together, connecting the heavens, the earth, and the underworld. For the Norse, Yggdrasil was the center of their world, and it symbolized the balance and order of the cosmos, showing how everything was interconnected.

Yggdrasil is often described as an immense ash tree, with a sturdy trunk, branches that seem to reach forever, and roots that extend into the most mysterious and faraway places. The tree connects the Nine Worlds of Norse mythology, which include places like Asgard, the realm of the gods; Midgard, the world of humans; and Hel, the underworld where the dead reside. Each of these worlds has its own unique characteristics, and Yggdrasil serves as the link that binds them all together, ensuring that the universe remains in harmony.

At the very top of Yggdrasil sits Asgard, home to the most powerful gods, including Odin, Thor, and Frigg. This is where the gods meet to discuss important matters and where Odin, the All-Father, often sits on his high throne to observe the entire world. Midgard, the world of humans, is located somewhere in the middle, while deep below, at the roots of the tree, lies the realm of Hel, where the souls of the dead reside. The vast branches of Yggdrasil even extend beyond the sky and into the unknown, making it a symbol of both life and mystery.

Yggdrasil's roots are just as important as its branches. These roots stretch into different places, each one linking the tree to a different part of the universe. One root reaches into Asgard, the home of the gods, and this root is associated with the Well of Urd, also known as the Well of Fate. The Norns, three mysterious women who control the destiny of all beings, live here. The Norns—Urd, Verdandi, and Skuld—are said to be the keepers of fate, spinning the threads of life for every human, god, and creature. Urd represents the past, Verdandi the present, and Skuld the future. They water Yggdrasil from the well, ensuring that the tree stays healthy and strong, which in turn keeps the balance of the universe intact.

Another root stretches into Jotunheim, the land of the giants, and here lies the Well of Mimir. Mimir was a wise being whose head was kept by Odin after Mimir's body was destroyed. Odin would often visit this well to seek knowledge and wisdom, as Mimir's head was said to contain all the secrets of the cosmos. It is at this well that Odin sacrificed one of his eyes in exchange for great wisdom, showing how highly the Norse gods valued knowledge and insight.

The third root reaches into Niflheim, a cold, dark, and misty realm. At this root lies the spring Hvergelmir, where many rivers flow out and bring life to different parts of the world. Niflheim is one of the oldest realms in Norse mythology and is often associated with cold, death, and the underworld. It's a place of deep mystery, and the waters of Hvergelmir play an important part in the cycle of life and death that Yggdrasil helps to maintain.

But Yggdrasil is not without its challenges. Even though it's a powerful tree that holds the universe together, it constantly faces threats. One of these threats comes from a dragon-like serpent named Nidhogg. Nidhogg lives at the base of the tree and gnaws on its roots, trying to weaken Yggdrasil. While the Norns work hard to keep the tree healthy by watering its roots, Nidhogg's constant chewing is a reminder that even something as strong as Yggdrasil is not indestructible. Nidhogg's gnawing represents the forces of destruction and chaos that exist in the world, showing that life is a delicate balance between creation and destruction.

Yggdrasil is also home to many other creatures. One of these is a giant eagle that sits at the top of the tree, overseeing the Nine Worlds.

Between the eagle's eyes is a hawk named Vedrfolnir, who watches over everything below. Meanwhile, at the base of the tree, along with Nidhogg, are four stags named Dainn, Dvalinn, Duneyrr, and Durathror. These stags roam the branches and nibble at the tree's leaves. Each of these creatures, whether they are helping or harming Yggdrasil, plays a role in the balance of the universe. There's even a squirrel named Ratatoskr that scurries up and down the tree, delivering messages—mostly insults—between the eagle at the top and Nidhogg at the roots. Ratatoskr's mischief reminds us that even in a world full of gods and powerful beings, there's room for humor and playful chaos.

Yggdrasil is not just a symbol of life but also of the cycle of time. According to Norse mythology, Yggdrasil will still stand even during Ragnarok, the end of the world. Ragnarok is a time when the gods will face a final battle against the giants, and much of the world will be destroyed. But even in the chaos and destruction of Ragnarok, Yggdrasil will not completely fall. It's said that after the destruction, two humans, Lif and Lifthrasir, will take shelter in Yggdrasil and survive the end of the world. They will emerge from the tree to start a new world, continuing the cycle of life once more. This shows how Yggdrasil represents not just the present world but the future as well, a symbol of renewal and hope even in the darkest times.

Yggdrasil also teaches an important lesson about balance. In Norse mythology, the gods, giants, humans, and other beings are all connected through the World Tree. Even though these different beings might be enemies, like the gods and the giants, they are still part of the same world, connected by Yggdrasil. The tree holds together forces of good and evil, light and darkness, life and death. It reminds us that these opposing forces are all necessary parts of the universe. Just as Yggdrasil's roots reach into both the well of life and the cold, dark underworld, life, too, is made up of both joy and sorrow, creation and destruction.

The importance of Yggdrasil in Norse mythology also extends to rituals and the everyday lives of the Norse people. They believed that the world was like Yggdrasil—a balance of interconnected forces. In ancient times, they would gather around sacred trees and groves, believing these natural places were connected to Yggdrasil. Some even believed that their ancestors' spirits lived within the trees, adding to the idea that Yggdrasil was not just a symbol of life in the mythological sense but also in a personal and spiritual one.

The image of Yggdrasil is still powerful today. Many people who study Norse mythology or follow ancient Norse traditions view the World Tree as a symbol of strength, resilience, and the interconnectedness of all things. Yggdrasil shows that life is a cycle, with birth, growth, decay, and renewal all part of the natural order. Even when things seem tough, like when Nidhogg is gnawing at its roots, Yggdrasil keeps standing, reminding us that balance and harmony are possible even in the face of hardship.

Yggdrasil's magic is not just in its size or its ability to connect the Nine Worlds but in what it represents for life, death, and everything in between. It's a symbol of the universe's complex web, a reminder that all things are connected, and that life, like the great tree, grows stronger when nurtured, yet it must always contend with forces that threaten to bring it down. Through Yggdrasil, the Norse myths teach us about the importance of wisdom, fate, and the cycles that make up our world. Whether it's the wise Norns, the mischievous squirrel, the gnawing dragon, or the brave humans who take shelter in the tree's embrace, Yggdrasil is the center of the Norse universe, and its magic touches every part of their stories.

The World Tree shows us that no matter how much chaos there is, no matter how much destruction or danger exists in the world, life will continue to grow, branch out, and reach toward the sky. The magic of Yggdrasil is not just in its immense size or its powerful roots, but in the way it ties the entire universe together, offering hope, balance, and the promise of renewal.

Chapter 4: The Heroic Adventures of Gilgamesh

The story of Gilgamesh is one of the oldest tales in the world, and it comes from ancient Mesopotamia, a place located between the Tigris and Euphrates Rivers, where some of the earliest human civilizations lived. The Epic of Gilgamesh, as it's called, was written thousands of years ago on clay tablets in a script called cuneiform, and it tells the heroic adventures of Gilgamesh, a mighty king who ruled the city of Uruk. But Gilgamesh wasn't just any ordinary king—he was said to be part god and part human, and his incredible strength and bravery made him a legendary figure. However, even though he was powerful and admired, Gilgamesh's story is about much more than just battles and victories. It's a story about friendship, love, the search for immortality, and what it means to be human.

Gilgamesh, as the story begins, is the king of Uruk, a massive and prosperous city. His kingdom is strong, and the city's walls, which he helped build, are tall and nearly indestructible. Yet, despite his greatness, Gilgamesh wasn't always the best ruler. He was known to be arrogant and harsh. He demanded too much from his people, taking whatever he wanted and ruling with little concern for others. The people of Uruk prayed to the gods to help them, asking for someone who could challenge their king and teach him a lesson.

The gods heard their prayers, and they created a wild man named Enkidu. Unlike Gilgamesh, who was raised in a palace, Enkidu lived in the wilderness among animals. He was strong, covered in hair, and knew nothing of civilization. Enkidu was a force of nature, pure and untamed, and he helped the animals by protecting them from hunters. But one day, a hunter saw Enkidu and realized that he would be a perfect match for Gilgamesh. He brought this news to the city, and soon Enkidu was introduced to the ways of humans.

A woman named Shamhat, who was a temple priestess, helped Enkidu by teaching him how to live like a man. She introduced him to food, drink, and clothing, and after spending time with her, Enkidu lost his wildness and became more human. He learned about the ways of society, and as he grew in knowledge, he heard tales of Gilgamesh. When he learned about how Gilgamesh mistreated the people of Uruk, he became furious. He decided to go to the city and confront this king, thinking that he could stop him.

When Enkidu arrived in Uruk, he challenged Gilgamesh to a fight. The two mighty figures battled fiercely. They wrestled, and neither one seemed to gain the upper hand at first. But as the fight went on, something unexpected happened—both Gilgamesh and Enkidu began to admire each other's strength and determination. Instead of one conquering the other, they became fast friends. Their bond of friendship became the heart of the story, and together, they went on many incredible adventures.

One of their first adventures was to confront a terrifying monster named Humbaba. Humbaba was the guardian of the Cedar Forest, a sacred place that the gods protected. He was a giant, and his face was so terrifying that just looking at him could fill someone with fear. Gilgamesh, however, was eager to prove his strength and bravery, so he and Enkidu set off to face Humbaba. When they entered the forest, they were filled with awe at its beauty, but they knew the real challenge was ahead.

The battle with Humbaba was fierce. The monster roared and threatened them, but Gilgamesh and Enkidu stood their ground. With the help of the god Shamash, who sent powerful winds to trap Humbaba, they were able to defeat him. Gilgamesh struck the final blow, and Humbaba's reign of terror over the forest came to an end. However, this victory wasn't without consequences. By killing Humbaba, they angered the gods, who had placed the monster in the forest to protect it. This act set in motion events that would change Gilgamesh's life forever.

After defeating Humbaba, Gilgamesh's fame grew even greater, and he was admired throughout the land. But soon, another challenge presented itself. The goddess Ishtar, who was the goddess of love and war, became infatuated with Gilgamesh and asked him to marry her. Gilgamesh, however, refused, knowing that many of Ishtar's previous lovers had met tragic fates. He insulted her, reminding her of how she had treated those who had loved her before. Furious at this rejection, Ishtar went to her father, Anu, the god of the heavens, and demanded that he send the Bull of Heaven to punish Gilgamesh.

The Bull of Heaven was a monstrous creature that caused great destruction wherever it went. It could create earthquakes with its steps and leave devastation in its wake. When the Bull of Heaven descended upon Uruk, it brought chaos, and the people of the city were terrified. But Gilgamesh and Enkidu, standing together, were determined to save their city. They fought the Bull of Heaven, and after a fierce battle, they managed to defeat it. Enkidu, in his triumph, tore off part of the bull and threw it at Ishtar, further enraging her.

The gods, now angered by the deaths of both Humbaba and the Bull of Heaven, decided that one of the two heroes had to be punished. Since it was Enkidu who had struck the final blow to the Bull of Heaven, the gods decreed that he must die. Enkidu soon fell ill, and despite Gilgamesh's efforts to save him, his friend's health deteriorated rapidly. As Enkidu lay dying, he cursed the day he was born, feeling betrayed by the gods who had once given him such strength and purpose. Gilgamesh stayed by his side, heartbroken and helpless, as his dearest friend slipped away.

The death of Enkidu was a turning point for Gilgamesh. He had always been strong, fearless, and confident, but the loss of his friend made him realize something he had never considered before—his own mortality. If even someone as powerful as Enkidu could die, then

Gilgamesh knew that he, too, would face death one day. This thought terrified him. Gilgamesh, who had spent his life conquering enemies and proving his strength, was now faced with a challenge he couldn't defeat: death.

Determined to find a way to avoid this fate, Gilgamesh set off on a new journey, one that would take him far from his city and into the unknown. He sought out Utnapishtim, a wise figure who had survived the great flood sent by the gods and had been granted immortality. Gilgamesh hoped that Utnapishtim could reveal the secret to eternal life, so that he could live forever and avoid the fate that had befallen Enkidu.

Gilgamesh's journey to find Utnapishtim was long and dangerous. He traveled through mountains, crossed deadly seas, and faced monsters along the way. At one point, he met Siduri, a tavern keeper who lived by the sea. Siduri offered Gilgamesh advice, telling him to enjoy life and accept the fate of humans. She reminded him that immortality was meant only for the gods and that humans should focus on living well instead of seeking endless life. But Gilgamesh, still mourning Enkidu and fearing death, wasn't ready to accept this wisdom.

Finally, Gilgamesh found Utnapishtim, who told him the story of the great flood. Utnapishtim had been chosen by the gods to survive when they decided to destroy humanity with a massive flood. He built a large boat, much like the story of Noah's Ark, and saved his family and animals from the floodwaters. After the flood, the gods rewarded him and his wife with immortality. But Utnapishtim explained to Gilgamesh that this gift was a one-time event, and no mortal could achieve it again.

Despite this, Utnapishtim offered Gilgamesh a test to prove his worthiness. He challenged Gilgamesh to stay awake for six days and seven nights. If he could do this, perhaps he could be granted immortality. But the test proved too difficult for Gilgamesh. Exhausted from his long journey, he quickly fell asleep. When he woke, Utnapishtim pointed out that even the greatest king could not conquer time and fatigue.

Before Gilgamesh left, Utnapishtim told him about a special plant that grew at the bottom of the sea. This plant was said to restore youth to anyone who ate it. Gilgamesh, still hopeful, found the plant and planned to take it back to Uruk to share its power with the people. But on his way home, as he rested by a pool of water, a snake crept up and stole the plant. The snake ate the plant and immediately shed its skin, becoming young again. Gilgamesh, devastated by this loss, realized that immortality had once again slipped out of his grasp.

With a heavy heart, Gilgamesh returned to Uruk. He had failed in his quest for eternal life, but through his journey, he learned an important lesson. He realized that while he couldn't escape death, he could still leave a lasting legacy. His deeds, his wisdom, and the city he built would live on after him, remembered by generations to come. He also came to understand that life's value wasn't in how long it lasted but in how it was lived. Gilgamesh accepted that all humans must face death, but by living with honor, courage, and love, they could make their lives truly meaningful.

In the end, Gilgamesh's heroic adventures weren't just about conquering monsters or seeking immortality—they were about discovering what it means to be human. His story is one of friendship, loss, and the realization that life is precious because it is finite. Though Gilgamesh was a king, part god and part man, his journey mirrors the struggles and hopes of all people, making his tale one of the most enduring and powerful stories in human history.

Chapter 5: The Egyptian God Ra's Journey

The Egyptian god Ra is one of the most important and powerful gods in ancient Egyptian mythology. He was the god of the sun, and the Egyptians believed that every day, he traveled across the sky, bringing light and warmth to the world. But Ra's journey wasn't just a simple trip from sunrise to sunset—it was a grand adventure, filled with challenges and dangers. The Egyptians believed that Ra's daily journey was essential to the survival of the world, and they told stories about the incredible journey he undertook each day to ensure that life could continue.

Ra was often depicted as a man with the head of a falcon, and atop his head, he wore a sun disk that represented the blazing sun. According to Egyptian mythology, Ra traveled in a magnificent boat, known as the "solar barque" or "sun boat." This boat carried Ra across the sky during the day and through the underworld at night. The Egyptians believed that the sky was like an ocean, and Ra's boat sailed across it, just like a ship on water. His journey across the sky symbolized the passing of time, with Ra bringing the sunrise in the morning, moving toward the zenith at noon, and descending into the horizon at dusk.

Each morning, when Ra rose from the eastern horizon, it marked the beginning of a new day. The Egyptians saw Ra as a creator god, responsible for bringing life to all things. As Ra traveled across the sky, his light touched the earth, making crops grow, warming the land, and sustaining life. The people would worship him and give thanks for the sunlight and the life it brought. Ra's presence in the sky was a sign of hope and protection, as he watched over both the gods and humans alike. His journey was seen as a daily renewal of life, and it symbolized the cycle of birth, growth, death, and rebirth.

But Ra's journey wasn't without its challenges. The Egyptians believed that during his nightly passage through the underworld, Ra faced numerous dangers, the most terrifying of which was the giant serpent Apophis. Apophis, also called Apep, was the god of chaos and darkness, and he hated Ra because Ra represented light and order. Every night, Apophis would try to stop Ra's journey by attacking the sun boat as it traveled through the underworld. Apophis was enormous, with a coiled body and sharp teeth, and his very presence threatened to plunge the world into eternal darkness.

The battle between Ra and Apophis was one of the most dramatic parts of Ra's journey. According to the myth, Ra wasn't alone in his fight against Apophis—he was accompanied by other gods who helped defend the sun boat. Some of these gods included Set, the god of storms and violence, who was one of Ra's fiercest protectors during the nightly battle. Set would use his strength and power to fight off Apophis, wielding weapons like spears and knives to pierce the serpent's massive body. Another key protector was the god Ma'at, the goddess of truth and order, who helped maintain balance in the universe. Ma'at's presence on the sun boat ensured that Ra's journey followed the natural order of things and that chaos would not prevail.

Apophis was a tricky and dangerous foe. He was able to use magic to try to stop Ra's boat, creating storms, throwing up waves of darkness, and trying to capsize the vessel. Sometimes, Apophis would swallow the sun boat, causing solar eclipses, when the sun seemed to disappear from the sky. The Egyptians believed that during these moments, Ra and his companions were locked in a fierce battle within Apophis, fighting to break free from the serpent's belly. The outcome of these battles was crucial because, if Apophis succeeded, the sun would never rise again, and the world would fall into eternal night.

But Ra was a determined and powerful god, and he always managed to defeat Apophis, even though the battle was fought every night. With the help of the other gods, Ra would slay the serpent, cutting through its thick scales and driving it back into the depths of the underworld. The Egyptians believed that each time Ra defeated Apophis, it was a triumph of light over darkness, good over evil, and order over chaos. The next morning, Ra would rise again in the eastern sky, victorious, and the cycle would start anew.

Ra's nightly journey through the underworld was more than just a battle with Apophis. It was also a symbolic journey of death and rebirth. In the underworld, Ra encountered the souls of the dead, as well as various gods and spirits who inhabited the realm of the afterlife. The Egyptians believed that Ra's light guided the souls of the dead, helping them navigate the darkness of the underworld and reach the afterlife. Ra's passage through the underworld was a reminder that death was not the end, but rather a part of the cycle of life. Just as Ra died each night and was reborn each morning, the souls of the dead could also be reborn into the afterlife if they lived according to Ma'at's principles of truth and justice.

One of the most important encounters Ra had during his nightly journey was with Osiris, the god of the dead and the ruler of the underworld. Osiris was a key figure in Egyptian mythology, representing resurrection and eternal life. When Ra met Osiris in the underworld, it symbolized the connection between the sun god's daily rebirth and the promise of life after death. The union of Ra and Osiris in the underworld was a powerful symbol of the eternal cycle of life, death, and renewal. This meeting ensured that not only the sun would rise again each day, but that the souls of the dead could find new life in the afterworld as well.

As Ra's boat continued its journey through the underworld, it passed through twelve gates, representing the twelve hours of the night. Each gate was guarded by fierce creatures and gods, and Ra had to overcome obstacles and face challenges at each one. These gates were symbolic of the different stages of the sun's journey and the passage of time. As the sun boat passed through the final gate, Ra would reach the horizon of the eastern sky, ready to rise again and bring a new day to the world.

The Egyptians viewed Ra's daily journey as a reflection of their own lives. Just as Ra faced challenges and overcame them, they believed that they, too, had to face the challenges of life with courage and faith. Ra's victory over Apophis was a reminder that light and goodness would always triumph over darkness and chaos, even in the most difficult times. His journey also reminded the Egyptians of the importance of balance and order in the world. They believed that by living in harmony with the principles of Ma'at—truth, justice, and order—they could ensure that Ra's journey would continue and that the world would remain safe from the forces of chaos.

Ra's journey wasn't just about his role as the sun god—it also connected him to other important gods in the Egyptian pantheon. For example, he was sometimes merged with the god Amun to become Amun-Ra, a powerful combination of two major deities. Amun-Ra was worshiped as the king of the gods and was considered the most powerful god in the Egyptian religion. Ra was also associated with Horus, the falcon-headed god of kingship and the sky, and Atum, the god of creation. These associations made Ra not only the god of the sun but also a symbol of creation, kingship, and divine power.

Ra's significance in Egyptian mythology is reflected in the temples and monuments built in his honor. The ancient Egyptians constructed enormous temples dedicated to Ra, particularly in the city of Heliopolis, which was the center of Ra's worship. Obelisks, tall stone pillars, were often erected in Ra's honor, symbolizing the rays of the sun and Ra's connection to the heavens. The great pyramids of Giza were also linked to Ra, as they were built to honor the pharaohs, who were believed to be the earthly representatives of Ra. The shape of the pyramids, with their pointed tops reaching toward the sky, was thought to represent the rays of the sun and the pharaoh's journey to join Ra in the afterlife.

In Egyptian art, Ra was often depicted sailing across the sky in his sun boat, with the sun disk shining brightly above him. He was sometimes shown as a falcon-headed god, a powerful and majestic symbol of his dominion over the skies. Other times, he was depicted as a full-bodied man with the head of a beetle (scarab), a creature that represented rebirth and regeneration. These images reflected Ra's dual role as both the giver of life and the force that brought about death and renewal.

The story of Ra's journey is more than just a myth—it was a central part of the ancient Egyptians' understanding of the universe and their place in it. Ra's daily battle against darkness and chaos, his victory over Apophis, and his passage through the underworld all symbolized the Egyptians' belief in the cycle of life, death, and rebirth. They saw Ra as the ultimate protector and creator, whose journey ensured that life could continue, that order would be maintained, and that even in death, there was the promise of renewal.

Through Ra's story, the ancient Egyptians found meaning and comfort in the cycles of nature, the rising and setting of the sun, and the eternal struggle between light and darkness. His journey, full of danger and triumph, reflected the challenges of life itself, reminding the people of Egypt that no matter how difficult the battle, the light of the sun would always return, bringing hope and new beginnings.

Chapter 6: The Tale of Maui and the Sun

The tale of Maui and the Sun is one of the most beloved stories in Polynesian mythology, and it tells the story of a clever and brave demigod named Maui. Maui is a hero in many Polynesian cultures, and his adventures are full of magic, trickery, and bravery. In this particular tale, Maui takes on an incredible challenge—to slow down the Sun itself. This story not only explains why the days are long enough for people to complete their tasks, but it also shows how Maui's cleverness and determination helped change the world for the better.

Maui was known for being a trickster and a hero, always thinking of ways to help people and solve problems. One day, he noticed that the Sun was moving too quickly across the sky. The days were too short, and the people didn't have enough time to finish their work. They couldn't fish, farm, or gather food before the Sun set. This caused great hardship, as they couldn't grow enough crops or catch enough fish to feed their families. The short days also made it difficult for them to enjoy life, as they didn't have time to rest or relax. Maui listened to their complaints and decided that something needed to be done.

Maui thought about the problem and came up with a bold idea—he would capture the Sun and slow it down. This was no small task. The Sun was a mighty and powerful force, and no one had ever dared to challenge it before. But Maui was determined, and he believed that with his cunning and strength, he could succeed. He knew that he would need some help, so he went to his brothers and told them of his plan. At first, his brothers were doubtful. How could anyone catch the Sun? But Maui convinced them that it was possible, and they agreed to help.

The first thing Maui needed was a strong rope. But not just any rope would do—it had to be magical and unbreakable. Maui's mother, Hina, was a goddess, and she was known for her skill in making fine and powerful things. Maui asked Hina if she could weave him a special rope that would be strong enough to hold the Sun. Hina agreed, and she spent days weaving a rope out of her own hair. The rope was long and thick, and it had magical properties that made it unbreakable. With the rope in hand, Maui was ready to put his plan into action.

Maui and his brothers traveled to the place where the Sun rose each morning. They journeyed for many days, climbing mountains and crossing valleys until they reached the spot where the Sun began its daily journey across the sky. The Sun was enormous and blindingly bright, but Maui was not afraid. He and his brothers worked quickly, weaving the rope into a giant net. They stretched the net across the path that the Sun would take, anchoring it to the ground with heavy stones. Then they hid, waiting for the Sun to rise.

As the first rays of sunlight appeared on the horizon, Maui and his brothers took their positions. The Sun, not knowing what was waiting for it, began to rise into the sky as it always did. But as it moved along its path, it became entangled in the net. The Sun struggled and pulled, trying to break free, but the net was too strong. Maui had caught the Sun!

With the Sun trapped, Maui emerged from his hiding place and approached it. The Sun was furious and demanded to be released. It thrashed and pulled at the net, trying to burn through it with its fiery heat, but the magical rope held fast. Maui, despite the intense heat, stood firm. He told the Sun that it had been moving too quickly across the sky, and that the people of the world didn't have enough time to do their work or enjoy their lives. The Sun, still angry, argued that it had always moved at the same speed, and that it wasn't its fault that the days were too short.

But Maui was clever, and he wasn't about to give up. He told the Sun that if it didn't slow down, he would never let it go. The Sun realized that it was trapped and had no choice but to listen to Maui. Reluctantly, the Sun agreed to Maui's demands. It would move more slowly across the sky, giving the people longer days to work, play, and rest. Maui, satisfied with this agreement, let the Sun go.

As the Sun rose higher into the sky, it began to move more slowly, just as it had promised. The days became longer, and the people rejoiced. They could now spend more time fishing, farming, and gathering food. They could complete their tasks without rushing and had time to enjoy life with their families and friends. The longer days brought prosperity and happiness to the people, and they were grateful to Maui for his bravery and cleverness.

Maui's victory over the Sun became one of his most famous feats, and it earned him a place as a great hero in Polynesian mythology. The story of how Maui tamed the Sun was told and retold by generations of people, reminding them of the power of determination and cleverness. Even though Maui was just one person, his actions had a huge impact on the world, making life better for everyone.

But Maui's adventure with the Sun didn't just explain why the days became longer—it also symbolized the balance between nature and humanity. In Polynesian culture, the natural world was full of powerful forces like the Sun, the ocean, and the wind, and these forces often seemed beyond human control. But through stories like Maui's, the people believed that with courage, intelligence, and persistence, even the most powerful forces of nature could be understood and influenced. Maui's story was a reminder that humans were not powerless in the face of the natural world, but rather, they could use their minds and skills to shape their environment and improve their lives.

The tale of Maui and the Sun also reflected the Polynesian belief in the importance of cooperation and teamwork. Although Maui was the hero of the story, he didn't capture the Sun by himself—he had the help of his brothers and the magic of his mother's rope. This showed that even the greatest challenges could be overcome when people worked together. Maui's brothers played a crucial role in setting the trap for the

Sun, and Hina's magical rope made the whole plan possible. Without their help, Maui's plan might have failed. This theme of cooperation and community was central to Polynesian culture, where people relied on each other for survival and success.

In some versions of the story, the Sun's agreement with Maui wasn't permanent. Over time, the Sun began to speed up again, and the days became shorter once more. This is why, in many parts of the world, the length of the days changes throughout the year. During the summer, the days are long and bright, while in the winter, the days are shorter and the nights are longer. The story of Maui and the Sun provided an explanation for these seasonal changes, showing how the natural world was constantly in motion and how even the forces of nature could change over time.

The tale of Maui and the Sun is not just a story about a clever trickster—it is a story about the power of determination, the importance of helping others, and the belief that even the greatest challenges can be overcome. Maui's courage in standing up to the Sun, his clever plan to trap it, and his success in making the world a better place made him a beloved hero in Polynesian culture. His story continues to be told today, inspiring people with the message that no challenge is too great if you use your mind, work together, and never give up.

Chapter 7: The Thunder of Zeus and the Olympians

The story of Zeus and the Olympians is one of the most powerful and exciting tales in Greek mythology. Zeus, the king of the gods, ruled from Mount Olympus, the highest mountain in Greece, and was known for his incredible power, wisdom, and authority. But one of the most remarkable aspects of Zeus was his control over thunder and lightning. Zeus was often depicted holding a thunderbolt, a mighty weapon that symbolized his strength and ability to command the forces of nature. The thunder of Zeus became a symbol of his dominance over both gods and mortals, and the stories surrounding him and the other Olympian gods are full of adventure, conflict, and larger-than-life battles.

Zeus was not born as the ruler of the gods; in fact, his journey to becoming the king of Olympus began with a struggle against his own father, Cronus. Cronus was one of the Titans, a race of powerful gods who ruled the universe before the Olympians. Cronus had been warned by a prophecy that one of his children would overthrow him, so he decided to swallow each of them as soon as they were born. One by one, Zeus's siblings—Hestia, Demeter, Hera, Hades, and Poseidon—were swallowed whole by Cronus. But when Zeus was born, his mother, Rhea, tricked Cronus by hiding the baby and giving him a stone wrapped in a blanket to swallow instead.

Zeus was raised in secret, hidden away in a cave on the island of Crete. There, he grew up strong and wise, and when he was old enough, he returned to confront his father. With the help of his grandmother, Gaia, the Earth goddess, Zeus tricked Cronus into drinking a potion that caused him to vomit up Zeus's siblings. Once freed, Zeus and his brothers and sisters joined forces to challenge Cronus and the Titans for control of the universe. This epic battle between the Olympians and the Titans was known as the Titanomachy.

The war was fierce, with both sides possessing great strength and power. The Titans, led by Cronus, fought with all their might, but Zeus had a secret weapon that gave him the upper hand: his thunderbolt. This thunderbolt was not just any weapon—it had been forged by the Cyclopes, one-eyed giants who were skilled blacksmiths. The Cyclopes had been imprisoned by Cronus, but Zeus freed them, and in gratitude, they gave him the thunderbolt. This magical weapon could summon the forces of the sky, calling down thunder, lightning, and storms to strike his enemies with incredible force.

With the thunderbolt in hand, Zeus unleashed his fury on the Titans. The sky was filled with the deafening roar of thunder, and flashes of lightning lit up the battlefield. Zeus's thunderbolt was so powerful that it could shatter mountains and shake the earth itself. One by one, the Titans were defeated, and Cronus was overthrown. Zeus and his siblings emerged victorious, and the era of the Titans came to an end.

After the war, Zeus and his brothers, Poseidon and Hades, divided the universe among themselves. Zeus became the ruler of the sky, Poseidon took control of the seas, and Hades became the god of the underworld. As the king of the gods, Zeus established his rule from Mount Olympus, where he and the other Olympian gods lived. From his throne on Olympus, Zeus watched over both the gods and humans, ensuring that order was maintained in the universe. But even though Zeus was a wise and just ruler, he was also known for his quick temper, and when he became angry, the thunder and lightning of Zeus could be terrifying.

One of the most famous stories about Zeus's thunder involves his punishment of the Titans who fought against him. After their defeat, Zeus banished the Titans to Tartarus, a deep and dark part of the underworld where they were imprisoned for eternity. Zeus placed powerful guards at the entrance to Tartarus to make sure that the Titans could never escape. But the Titans were not the only ones to feel the wrath of Zeus's thunder. Throughout Greek mythology, Zeus used his thunderbolt to punish mortals and gods who disobeyed him or threatened the balance of the universe.

One such story is the tale of Prometheus, a Titan who defied Zeus by giving fire to humans. Prometheus loved humanity and wanted to help them, so he stole fire from the gods and brought it to Earth, teaching people how to use it for warmth, cooking, and building. This act of defiance enraged Zeus, who had forbidden the gods from sharing such knowledge with mortals. As punishment, Zeus used his thunderbolt to strike Prometheus and chained him to a rock on a mountaintop. There, every day, an eagle would come and eat Prometheus's liver, which would grow back each night, so that his suffering continued endlessly. Prometheus was eventually freed by the hero Heracles, but his punishment served as a warning of the consequences of defying the will of Zeus.

Zeus's thunderbolt was also used to settle conflicts among the gods. In Greek mythology, the gods were often involved in disputes and quarrels, and Zeus, as their king, had to maintain order among them. One famous example of this is the story of the Trojan War. The gods took sides in the war between the Greeks and the Trojans, and their interference often caused chaos on the battlefield. Zeus, however, remained neutral for much of the war, using his thunderbolt to remind the other gods that he was in charge. When the gods' meddling became too much, Zeus would hurl his thunderbolt, causing them to retreat and remember their place. His power over the other gods made it clear that no one, not even the gods of Olympus, could challenge Zeus's authority.

But Zeus's thunderbolt wasn't just a symbol of punishment and wrath—it was also a tool of protection. Zeus was often called upon to protect both gods and mortals from danger, and his thunderbolt was the ultimate weapon in these battles. One such story involves the monster Typhon, a fearsome creature born of Gaia and Tartarus. Typhon was so enormous and powerful that he threatened to destroy the gods and take over the universe. His body was covered in serpents, and he could breathe fire, making him nearly unstoppable.

The gods were terrified of Typhon, and many of them fled to Egypt, disguising themselves as animals to escape his wrath. But Zeus stood his ground, determined to protect Olympus and the world from this monstrous threat. In an epic battle, Zeus faced Typhon, hurling his thunderbolts with all his might. The sky lit up with flashes of lightning, and the roar of thunder echoed across the land. Zeus struck Typhon with his thunderbolt again and again, until the monster was finally defeated. Zeus then trapped Typhon under Mount Etna, a volcano in Sicily, where it was said that Typhon's rage could still be felt in the form of volcanic eruptions.

The thunderbolt of Zeus also played a role in stories of love and romance. While Zeus was known for his many love affairs, both with goddesses and mortal women, his thunderbolt was sometimes used to win the affection of those he desired. In one story, Zeus fell in love with the beautiful mortal Semele, the daughter of the king of Thebes. Semele became pregnant with Zeus's child, but she was unaware that Zeus was a god. Hera, Zeus's wife, became jealous of Semele and tricked her into asking Zeus to reveal his true form.

Zeus had promised Semele that he would grant her any wish, and although he knew it was dangerous, he could not break his promise. When Zeus revealed himself in all his divine glory, the sight was too much for a mortal to bear. The power of his thunder and lightning consumed Semele, and she perished in the flames. However, Zeus managed to save their unborn child, the god Dionysus, who would later become the god of wine and revelry. This story showed that while Zeus's thunderbolt was a source of great power, it could also be dangerous and uncontrollable, even to those he loved.

Throughout Greek mythology, Zeus's thunder and lightning represented his ultimate authority and power over the universe. Whether he was punishing those who defied him, protecting the world from monstrous threats, or maintaining order among the gods, Zeus's thunderbolt was a symbol of his control over both nature and the divine. It was said that when thunder roared and lightning flashed in the sky, it was a sign that Zeus was watching, reminding both gods and mortals of his presence and power.

Zeus's thunderbolt became one of the most iconic symbols in all of Greek mythology, and it was often invoked in prayers and sacrifices. People would pray to Zeus for protection, justice, and mercy, believing that his thunderbolt could bring both blessings and punishment. Temples were built in his honor, and statues of Zeus often depicted him holding the thunderbolt, ready to strike down any who threatened the order of the world. As the king of the gods, Zeus's role was to keep balance and harmony in the universe, and his thunderbolt was the tool that allowed him to do so.

The thunder of Zeus was more than just a weapon—it was a symbol of the cosmic order that the ancient Greeks believed in. It represented the balance between chaos and order, between the natural world and the divine. Zeus, as the king of the gods, was the guardian of this balance, using his thunderbolt to ensure that the universe remained in harmony. Through his power, wisdom, and control over the forces of nature, Zeus became not only the ruler of the gods but also a symbol of justice and authority for all who believed in him.

In the end, the tale of Zeus and his thunderbolt is one of triumph, power, and the protection of the universe. His thunder echoed through the myths of ancient Greece, and his reign as king of the Olympians was marked by both moments of fierce battle and divine leadership. Whether he was facing down Titans, monsters, or rebellious gods, Zeus's thunderbolt ensured that he remained the undisputed ruler of Olympus and the protector of the world.

Chapter 8: The Dreamtime of the Aboriginal Ancestors

The Dreamtime is one of the most important and fascinating aspects of Aboriginal culture in Australia. It is a concept that goes beyond just stories; it's a way of understanding the world, the land, and the people who live on it. For the Aboriginal peoples, the Dreamtime isn't just something that happened long ago—it is always present, connecting the past, the present, and the future. The stories of the Dreamtime explain how the land was shaped, how animals and people came to be, and how everything in the world is interconnected. The Dreamtime also teaches important lessons about respect for the land, the animals, and each other.

According to Aboriginal belief, in the very beginning, the world was formless and empty. There was no land, no animals, no people, and no plants. The earth was flat and lifeless, waiting for something to bring it to life. This time before creation is often referred to as the "Dreaming." Then, out of the darkness, the ancestral spirits began to emerge. These were powerful beings, often taking the form of giant animals, plants, or human-like creatures with extraordinary abilities. These ancestors had the power to shape the world, and as they traveled across the land, they created everything we see today—rivers, mountains, forests, deserts, and even the stars in the sky.

As the ancestral spirits moved through the empty world, they gave life to the land. Some of the most well-known ancestors include the Rainbow Serpent, the Quinkins, the Wanjina, and Baiame. The Rainbow Serpent, for example, is one of the most important figures in many Aboriginal cultures. It is said that the Rainbow Serpent slithered across the land, creating rivers, valleys, and mountains as it moved. Wherever the serpent traveled, it left behind waterholes, which became vital sources of life for the plants, animals, and people that would come later. The Rainbow Serpent is also seen as a protector of the land and its people, but it can be dangerous if disrespected, bringing floods or droughts.

Other Dreamtime stories talk about how different animals came into being. In one story, Tiddalik the frog drank all the water in the land, causing a terrible drought. The other animals were desperate to find water, and they tried everything they could to make Tiddalik laugh, hoping that if he laughed, he would spill the water back onto the earth. After many failed attempts, a small eel finally made Tiddalik laugh, and the water was released, saving all the creatures. Stories like this one not only explain natural phenomena, like droughts and floods, but also teach important lessons about cooperation, patience, and problem-solving.

The Dreamtime is also closely tied to the Aboriginal understanding of the land. To the Aboriginal people, the land is not just a place to live—it is a living, breathing part of their culture and identity. Every rock, tree, and river have a story that connects it to the ancestors and the Dreamtime. These stories are passed down from generation to generation through songs, dances, paintings, and oral storytelling. They are not written down in books, but instead, they live in the minds and hearts of the Aboriginal people, and they are shared through ceremonies and rituals that keep the Dreamtime alive.

One of the most important concepts in the Dreamtime is the idea of "songlines." Songlines are the paths that the ancestors traveled as they moved across the land, creating the world. Each songline tells the story of a specific ancestor and their journey, and the songs themselves contain detailed knowledge about the land. The Aboriginal people use these songs to navigate the landscape, and they can follow a songline across vast distances, knowing exactly where to find water, food, and shelter. In this way, the songlines serve as both a map and a story, guiding the people both physically and spiritually.

In the Dreamtime stories, the ancestors not only created the physical landscape, but they also gave life to the animals and the people. The first humans were created by the ancestors, and they were given the knowledge they needed to survive on the land. The ancestors taught them how to hunt, gather food, make tools, and perform ceremonies to honor the spirits. The Dreamtime also established the laws that the Aboriginal people follow, known as the "Dreaming laws." These laws guide how people should live, how they should treat each other, and how they should care for the land. They emphasize respect, balance, and harmony with nature.

The Dreamtime stories are incredibly diverse, as there are many different Aboriginal groups across Australia, each with their own unique traditions and beliefs. Some groups live in the deserts of the interior, while others live along the coast or in the forests. Each group has its own version of the Dreamtime stories, shaped by the environment in which they live. For example, coastal groups might have Dreamtime stories about the sea and marine animals, while desert groups might have stories about the kangaroos, emus, and other animals that live in the dry interior. Despite these differences, all the stories share a common theme: the connection between the people, the land, and the ancestors.

One of the central ideas in the Dreamtime is that time is cyclical. This means that the past, present, and future are not separate—they are all interconnected. The ancestors created the world in the Dreamtime, but their spirits are still present today, watching over the land and the people. Every time the Aboriginal people perform a ceremony, sing a songline, or tell a Dreamtime story, they are connecting with the ancestors and keeping the Dreamtime alive. This sense of timelessness gives the Dreamtime stories a deep spiritual significance. They are not just myths or legends—they are living, breathing parts of Aboriginal culture that continue to guide the people in their everyday lives.

One of the most important ceremonies in Aboriginal culture is the corroboree, which is a gathering where people come together to sing, dance, and tell stories from the Dreamtime. During a corroboree, the participants paint their bodies with special designs, representing the ancestors and the animals of the Dreamtime. The songs and dances are performed in a specific order, following the stories of the ancestors as they moved through the land. The corroboree is a way of honoring the ancestors, passing down knowledge to the younger generations, and maintaining the connection between the people and the Dreamtime.

The Dreamtime also has a strong connection to the Aboriginal art. Aboriginal artists often create paintings that depict the stories of the Dreamtime, using dots, lines, and symbols to represent the ancestors, the animals, and the landscape. These paintings are not just beautiful works of art—they are visual representations of the Dreamtime stories, capturing the knowledge and wisdom of the ancestors. The colors and patterns in the paintings are carefully chosen, and each symbol has a specific meaning. For example, a spiral might represent a waterhole, while a series of dots could represent a journey across the land. These paintings are often created on bark, rocks, or sand, and they are an important part of Aboriginal culture and storytelling.

The Dreamtime stories are also a way of explaining the natural world. For the Aboriginal people, everything in nature has a spirit, and the Dreamtime stories explain how these spirits came to be. For example, the story of the Rainbow Serpent explains why rivers wind across the land, and the story of the sun and the moon explains the cycles of day and night. These stories are not just explanations of natural phenomena—they also teach important lessons about respect for the environment. The Aboriginal people believe that if they take care of the land, the spirits of the Dreamtime will continue to protect and provide for them.

In many ways, the Dreamtime is a way of understanding the world that is very different from Western ideas of history and science. In

Western culture, history is often seen as a series of events that happened in the past, and science explains how the natural world works. But for the Aboriginal people, the Dreamtime is not just about the past—it is a living, ongoing part of their culture. The stories of the Dreamtime are not just myths or legends—they are a way of understanding the world and the people's place in it. The Dreamtime teaches that everything is connected: the land, the animals, the people, and the ancestors are all part of the same web of life.

The Dreamtime also emphasizes the importance of balance and harmony. In the Dreamtime stories, the ancestors created the world in a state of balance, where everything had its place and purpose. The animals, plants, and humans were all part of this balance, and it was the responsibility of the people to maintain it. This idea of balance is central to Aboriginal culture, and it is reflected in the way the people interact with the land. They take only what they need, and they give back to the land through ceremonies, rituals, and respect for the natural world.

In conclusion, the Dreamtime is a deeply spiritual and complex aspect of Aboriginal culture. It is more than just a collection of stories—it is a way of understanding the world, the land, and the people's place in it. The Dreamtime explains how the world was created, how the ancestors shaped the land, and how everything is connected. It teaches important lessons about respect, balance, and harmony with nature. For the Aboriginal people, the Dreamtime is not just a distant memory—it is a living, ongoing part of their culture, passed down from generation to generation through stories, songs, dances, and art. Through the Dreamtime, the Aboriginal people maintain their connection to the land, the ancestors, and the spirits of the world around them.

Chapter 9: The Mysterious Phoenix of Ancient China

In ancient China, the Phoenix, also known as the Fenghuang, is one of the most mystical and revered creatures in Chinese mythology. The Phoenix is not like the Western idea of a fiery bird that dies in flames and is reborn from its ashes. In Chinese mythology, it represents peace, prosperity, and harmony. The Phoenix is a symbol of beauty, grace, and transformation, and it is often linked to the concept of balance. In many ways, the Phoenix embodies the ideal union of yin and yang, the two complementary forces that keep the universe in harmony.

The Phoenix, or Fenghuang, is often described as a magnificent bird with bright, multicolored feathers. Its body is a blend of various birds and animals, such as a peacock, a pheasant, a rooster, and sometimes even elements of a dragon. The Phoenix's physical description is as much about symbolism as it is about its appearance. Each part of the Phoenix's body represents something meaningful. For example, its head is like a pheasant, symbolizing virtue, while its back is like a tortoise, representing strength. Its tail feathers are said to be as vibrant as the sun, and its wings are strong enough to fly to the heavens.

In Chinese culture, the Phoenix is often paired with the dragon, and together, they represent a perfect union. The dragon, a symbol of power and masculinity, complements the Phoenix, which stands for grace, femininity, and beauty. When they are shown together in Chinese art, it symbolizes the harmonious relationship between husband and wife or between two opposing forces that, when balanced, bring harmony to the universe. In ancient times, the dragon and the Phoenix were commonly used in imperial symbolism, with the dragon representing the emperor and the Phoenix representing the empress. The union of these two creatures reflected the harmony needed to rule a prosperous and peaceful kingdom.

The Phoenix is also a creature of great moral standing in Chinese mythology. It is said to appear only during times of peace and prosperity and would never be seen during times of chaos or war. The arrival of the Phoenix was believed to be a good omen, signaling that the emperor was ruling wisely and that the land was in balance. In ancient China, the Phoenix was also associated with the virtues of kindness, fairness, and righteousness. It was believed that if a ruler displayed these virtues, the Phoenix would bless the land with its presence, ensuring a time of great prosperity and harmony.

According to legend, the Phoenix lives for an incredibly long time. Some myths say it lives for a thousand years before retreating to its nest, where it dies in a blaze of flames, only to be reborn again. However, this version of the story is more common in other cultures, such as in ancient Egypt and Greece, than in China. In Chinese mythology, the Phoenix is less about death and rebirth and more about longevity, peace, and eternal life. Its immortality is a reflection of its divine nature, as it is seen as a celestial bird that can live through the ages without ever perishing.

One of the most interesting aspects of the Phoenix in Chinese mythology is its connection to the natural world. The Phoenix is said to have dominion over all birds, and it is often referred to as the "King of Birds." It is believed to have the power to communicate with nature, particularly the wind and the trees. In some stories, the Phoenix is depicted as having the ability to bring rain during times of drought or to calm storms with its presence. Because of this, the Phoenix was often seen as a guardian of nature and the environment. Its ability to control the elements was thought to maintain the balance between heaven and earth.

In addition to its association with nature, the Phoenix is also linked to the five virtues in Chinese philosophy: benevolence, righteousness, propriety, wisdom, and sincerity. The Phoenix embodies these virtues, and its presence was believed to inspire people to act with kindness and fairness. It was said that the Phoenix would only appear in places where virtue was upheld, and its absence was seen as a warning that moral decay or corruption had taken root. The Phoenix was, therefore, not just a symbol of good fortune but also a reminder of the importance of living a virtuous life.

The Phoenix is deeply connected to Chinese cosmology as well. In traditional Chinese thought, the universe is made up of five elements: wood, fire, earth, metal, and water. The Phoenix is most closely associated with the element of fire, which represents energy, life, and transformation. In some versions of the legend, the Phoenix is said to be born from the flames, much like the Western version of the bird. Its connection to fire also represents the light and warmth that the sun brings to the world, allowing plants to grow, animals to thrive, and people to live in prosperity.

Throughout Chinese history, the Phoenix has also played an important role in art and architecture. The image of the Phoenix can be found on everything from ancient pottery and jewelry to grand palaces and temples. The Phoenix was often carved into imperial thrones or painted on the walls of royal chambers, representing the empress and the ideal virtues of the court. Its beauty and grace made it a popular subject in traditional Chinese paintings, where it is often shown soaring through the sky with outstretched wings, surrounded by clouds and sunlight.

In addition to its symbolic role, the Phoenix also appears in many traditional Chinese stories and myths. In one famous tale, the Phoenix is said to have helped the legendary Yellow Emperor, one of the first rulers of China, to conquer his enemies and unite the land. The Phoenix guided the emperor to victory, bringing peace to the kingdom. This story illustrates the belief that the Phoenix not only symbolizes peace but also has the power to bring it about through its divine intervention.

The Phoenix also holds a special place in Chinese celebrations and festivals. During the Lunar New Year, which is the most important festival in China, images of the Phoenix can often be seen decorating homes and public spaces. The Phoenix is believed to bring good luck, and its presence during the New Year celebrations is a wish for prosperity, happiness, and peace in the coming year. In wedding ceremonies, the Phoenix is often included in the decorations, symbolizing the harmonious union of the bride and groom.

In modern China, the Phoenix continues to be a powerful symbol. It is often used in business logos, fashion designs, and cultural events, representing strength, grace, and resilience. The image of the Phoenix has even been adopted as a symbol of Chinese women, embodying their beauty, strength, and wisdom. The Phoenix's association with the empress and feminine power makes it an enduring symbol of women's leadership and empowerment.

In some regions of China, the Phoenix is also linked to specific places or landmarks. Certain mountains or rivers are said to be the home of the Phoenix, and these areas are considered sacred. Pilgrims and travelers would visit these sites, hoping to catch a glimpse of the legendary bird or to receive its blessings. The idea that the Phoenix resides in special, sacred places further adds to its mystical and mysterious nature.

Over time, the Phoenix has come to represent not only the ideals of Chinese culture but also the idea of transformation and renewal. In times of great hardship or challenge, the Phoenix is seen as a symbol of hope and rebirth. Just as the Phoenix can rise from the ashes, people too can overcome difficulties and emerge stronger and more beautiful. This idea of resilience is one of the reasons why the Phoenix has remained such a beloved and enduring symbol throughout Chinese history.

In conclusion, the Phoenix, or Fenghuang, is one of the most magical and revered creatures in Chinese mythology. Its beauty, grace, and strength have made it a symbol of peace, harmony, and prosperity. The Phoenix is more than just a mythical bird—it embodies the virtues of kindness, wisdom, and fairness. It is deeply connected to the natural world, the elements, and Chinese cosmology, representing the balance between heaven and earth. The Phoenix's presence brings good fortune, and its absence warns of chaos and moral decay. Through its stories, art, and symbolism, the Phoenix continues to inspire and captivate the imaginations of people, making it one of the most mysterious and enduring figures in Chinese culture.

Chapter 10: The Underworld Voyage of Izanagi

The story of Izanagi's voyage to the underworld is one of the most captivating and dramatic tales in Japanese mythology. It is a journey filled with emotion, danger, and supernatural encounters, and it holds deep cultural and spiritual significance. Izanagi, along with his wife Izanami, are considered the creators of the world in Japanese myth. They were responsible for forming the islands of Japan, and they gave birth to many of the gods and creatures that populate Japanese myth. However, their story takes a tragic turn when Izanami dies, leading Izanagi on a perilous journey to the land of the dead, known as Yomi, to bring her back.

According to the myth, Izanagi and Izanami were tasked by the gods to create the world. Using a jeweled spear, they stirred the oceans, and from the foam, the first landmass was formed. This land became the islands of Japan, and the two gods settled there to continue their work of creation. Together, they gave birth to many gods and goddesses who ruled over various aspects of nature and human life. However, when Izanami gave birth to the fire god Kagutsuchi, the intense heat of the newborn god severely burned her, causing her death. Stricken with grief, Izanagi was unwilling to accept her loss and decided to descend into the underworld to retrieve her.

Yomi, the Japanese underworld, is a dark and shadowy place, much different from the world of the living. In Yomi, there is no light, no warmth, and the dead reside there for eternity. It is a place of stagnation, where souls lose their former beauty and vitality. Yomi is described as a land of gloom and decay, a stark contrast to the vibrant and dynamic world that Izanagi and Izanami had created together. The journey to Yomi was not one that could be taken lightly, and by choosing to enter the land of the dead, Izanagi was stepping into a place from which very few ever returned.

As Izanagi made his way into Yomi, he found the entrance guarded by a large boulder that blocked the path between the living and the dead. However, determined to save his beloved wife, Izanagi moved past the barrier and entered the underworld. Upon finding Izanami, he pleaded with her to return with him to the world of the living. Izanami, however, explained that she had already eaten the food of Yomi, which bound her to the land of the dead. In many cultures, including Japanese mythology, consuming food in the underworld is a binding act that ties a soul to the realm of the dead forever. Yet, despite this, Izanami promised to speak to the rulers of Yomi and ask for permission to leave.

Izanami warned Izanagi to wait for her and not to look at her until she returned, but after waiting for a long time, Izanagi grew impatient. Worried and eager to see his wife, he ignored her warning and lit a small comb from his hair as a torch to look for her. What he saw shocked him to his core. Izanami's once-beautiful form had decayed, and she had become a rotting corpse crawling with maggots and other foul creatures. Overcome with horror and sorrow, Izanagi fled in terror, realizing that his wife was no longer the radiant goddess he had once known. In that moment, Izanami was filled with rage at his betrayal and the broken promise, and she sent the foul spirits of Yomi to chase after him and drag him back to the underworld.

Izanagi's escape from Yomi was a frantic race against the forces of the dead. He ran as fast as he could, pursued by the vengeful spirits, and eventually reached the entrance to the underworld. In desperation, he grabbed the boulder that had once blocked the entrance and sealed it, trapping the spirits inside. This act created a permanent separation between the living world and the world of the dead, ensuring that the two realms would never again mix. From that point on, Yomi was a place that the living could not enter without grave consequences, and the dead would remain forever in their shadowy world.

As Izanagi stood at the entrance to Yomi, he heard the furious voice of Izanami from behind the sealed boulder. In her anger, she vowed that she would kill one thousand people every day as revenge for his betrayal. Saddened by her words, Izanagi replied that he would ensure that one thousand five hundred people were born every day, ensuring that life would always overcome death. This exchange marked the beginning of the cycle of life and death, a theme that is deeply embedded in Japanese culture. It reflects the balance between creation and destruction, and the eternal cycle that governs both the world of the living and the underworld.

After his harrowing escape from Yomi, Izanagi was overcome with feelings of impurity and sorrow from his encounter with death. In Japanese culture, death is considered a source of pollution, and contact with the dead brings a spiritual uncleanliness that must be cleansed. To purify himself, Izanagi performed a ritual cleansing, or "misogi," in a river. As he washed away the impurities of Yomi, new gods and goddesses were born from his actions. It was during this purification that three of the most important deities in Japanese mythology were born from Izanagi's body. From his left eye came Amaterasu, the sun goddess who would become the ruler of the heavens. From his right eye came Tsukuyomi, the moon god who ruled the night. And from his nose came Susanoo, the storm god who governed the seas and storms.

These three gods, born from Izanagi's purification, became central figures in Japanese mythology. Amaterasu, in particular, is one of the most revered deities, as she is considered the ancestor of the Japanese imperial family and the goddess who brings light to the world. The creation of these gods from Izanagi's cleansing ritual symbolizes the idea of renewal and transformation. Even after the sorrow and horror of his journey to the underworld, Izanagi was able to create new life and restore balance to the world.

The story of Izanagi's voyage to the underworld also has deep connections to the Shinto religion, which is the indigenous spiritual belief system of Japan. In Shinto, purity and cleanliness are essential, and rituals of purification are performed to cleanse oneself of spiritual impurities. Izanagi's purification after his return from Yomi is a reflection of this belief, and it highlights the importance of maintaining spiritual purity in the face of death and decay.

The myth of Izanagi and Izanami also reflects the human experience of love, loss, and the inevitability of death. Izanagi's grief at losing Izanami and his desperate attempt to bring her back from the underworld are emotions that many people can relate to. His journey to Yomi symbolizes the lengths we go to in order to hold on to those we love, even when faced with the finality of death. However, his realization that he cannot save Izanami, and his eventual acceptance of her transformation, is a powerful reminder of the natural cycle of life and death.

In some versions of the myth, Izanami is transformed into a fearsome deity of death after her rejection by Izanagi. She becomes the ruler of Yomi, and it is said that she waits there, holding a grudge against the living world. This transformation represents the idea that death, once embraced, becomes a force of its own. Izanami, once a goddess of creation, becomes a figure associated with the destruction and decay that comes with death. Her vow to take one thousand lives each day is a reminder that death is an inescapable part of life, but Izanagi's promise to bring more life into the world shows that creation and life will always continue, despite death's presence.

The story of Izanagi's voyage to the underworld is a tale of creation, destruction, love, loss, and renewal. It is a foundational myth in Japanese culture, illustrating the balance between life and death, and the importance of purification and spiritual renewal. The themes of this myth—grief, betrayal, and the inevitable separation between the living and the dead—are universal, and they resonate with people across cultures and generations. Through Izanagi's journey, we see the profound connections between the natural world, the spiritual realm, and the cycles that govern life itself.

Chapter 11: The Coyote's Clever Tricks in American Lore

In Native American mythology, Coyote is one of the most fascinating and complex figures. Known as the Trickster, Coyote appears in many stories across various Native American cultures, particularly in the western parts of North America. He is a creature of mischief, wit, and often chaos, but he also plays an important role in shaping the world and teaching valuable lessons. Unlike some of the more noble or heroic characters in mythology, Coyote is flawed—he is greedy, selfish, and often foolish—but that's what makes his stories so entertaining and relatable. Through his clever tricks and misadventures, Coyote reflects the imperfections of humanity, and even though he frequently causes trouble, there is usually wisdom to be gained from his actions.

One of the main characteristics of Coyote is his cleverness. He is always thinking up schemes and tricks, whether it's to get food, escape danger, or simply have a good laugh at someone else's expense. In many stories, Coyote outsmarts more powerful animals and even gods with his cunning. However, his tricks don't always work out as planned, and sometimes his cleverness backfires on him, causing more trouble than he intended. This mix of success and failure makes Coyote a very human-like figure, as he is always trying to get ahead but often ends up in difficult situations due to his own greed or arrogance.

In one famous story from the Nez Perce people, Coyote plays a trick to steal fire for humans. Long ago, humans were cold and shivered through the nights because they didn't have fire. The fire was kept by a group of Fire Beings who lived far away, and they refused to share it with anyone. Determined to help the humans, Coyote came up with a clever plan. He decided to sneak into the camp of the Fire Beings and steal a burning coal. Coyote was fast and agile, but the Fire Beings were always watching their fire closely, so he knew he couldn't simply walk up and take it. Instead, he enlisted the help of his animal friends, including Eagle, Squirrel, and Frog.

Coyote told his friends to stand in a long line, each one ready to take the fire and pass it along. He then crept into the Fire Beings' camp while they were distracted. With great stealth, Coyote snatched a piece of burning coal and ran as fast as he could. The Fire Beings quickly realized what had happened and gave chase. Coyote passed the fire to Squirrel, who raced up a tree, then to Eagle, who soared high into the sky. Each animal carried the fire a little further until it reached Frog, who hid the coal in his mouth and jumped into a stream to put out the flames chasing after them. Thanks to Coyote's clever plan, the fire was delivered safely to humans, and they were finally able to stay warm. However, the story didn't end without a cost. Squirrel's tail became crooked from carrying the hot coal, and Frog lost its voice after holding the fire in its mouth for so long. These lasting changes show how even Coyote's successful tricks often come with consequences.

Another well-known tale involving Coyote's tricks comes from the Crow people and explains the origin of buffalo. According to the story, there was once a time when humans had no buffalo to hunt. The buffalo lived far away, hidden behind a giant cliff, and the people were starving. Coyote, always the one to find a way out of trouble, came up with a plan to release the buffalo. He asked the rock that held the buffalo captive to open up, promising that he wouldn't let any of them escape. The rock agreed, and the buffalo began to pour out, one by one.

As the buffalo emerged, Coyote couldn't resist playing a trick. He shouted, "Run free!" and encouraged the buffalo to break away from the rock's grip. The buffalo charged out, stampeding across the plains, and soon there were too many for Coyote to control. The buffalo became wild and spread all over the land, making it impossible for the rock to call them back. The humans were thrilled to have the buffalo, but the rock was furious at Coyote for breaking his promise. To punish him, the rock chased Coyote and eventually crushed his tail. This story, like many Coyote tales, ends with a mix of success and punishment. While Coyote succeeded in freeing the buffalo, his trick caused him personal harm.

Coyote's tricks often serve as a way to explain natural phenomena or important cultural practices. In some stories, his cleverness leads to the creation of the stars, the rivers, or even certain animals. However, his actions are rarely straightforward. Instead of being a noble creator who sets out to make the world a better place, Coyote is usually motivated by selfish desires, such as hunger, laziness, or a desire to prove his superiority. It's only by accident or through unintended consequences that his tricks result in something beneficial. This dual nature of Coyote as both a troublemaker and a creator makes him a unique figure in mythology, as he exists in the gray area between hero and villain.

In another story, from the Navajo people, Coyote's tricks involve stealing water from a group of water spirits. At the time, the water spirits controlled all the water in the world and refused to share it with the humans. This made life very difficult, as people were constantly thirsty and could not grow crops. Coyote, seeing the humans' suffering, decided to take action. He sneaked into the water spirits' domain and stole their water jars. Coyote distributed the water to the rivers and streams, ensuring that humans would have enough to drink. However, in his haste, Coyote spilled some of the water, which created the deserts. In this story, Coyote's trick was meant to help humanity, but his carelessness also led to the creation of harsh, dry landscapes where water is still scarce.

Coyote's tricks aren't always successful, and sometimes his actions lead to disasters. In some tales, Coyote's greed or arrogance causes him to be humiliated or even killed, only to be resurrected later. His death and rebirth cycle make him an eternal figure in mythology—no matter how many times he is punished, he always comes back, ready for his next scheme. In one such story, Coyote challenges a group of gods to a race, thinking that his speed will allow him to win easily. However, the gods trick him by leading him on a long and dangerous path, filled with traps and obstacles. Coyote, overconfident as always, falls into a pit and is killed. Yet, after some time passes, Coyote is reborn, and he immediately begins plotting his next adventure, having learned nothing from his previous mistakes.

Through his clever tricks, Coyote often reveals deeper truths about human nature. His stories show how intelligence and resourcefulness can help overcome challenges, but they also warn against the dangers of arrogance, greed, and dishonesty. Coyote's actions reflect the complexities of life, where even the best-laid plans can go wrong, and where the line between success and failure is often blurred. Despite his flaws, Coyote is a beloved character in Native American mythology because he embodies the spirit of survival and adaptability. He shows that even when things don't go as planned, there is always a way to bounce back and try again.

Coyote's cleverness also makes him a figure of resistance and rebellion. In many stories, he challenges the gods or other powerful figures who hoard resources or impose unfair rules. Coyote's tricks often involve redistributing power or resources, whether it's stealing fire, water, or food for humans. In this way, he is a champion for the underdog, using his wits to outsmart those who would otherwise keep power for themselves. His rebellious nature is one of the reasons why Coyote is so appealing—he refuses to accept the world as it is and constantly seeks to change it, even if his methods are unorthodox.

The lessons that come from Coyote's clever tricks vary from story to story. In some tales, the lesson is about the importance of sharing, as seen in the stories where Coyote steals fire or water for humanity. In others, the lesson is about humility, as Coyote often suffers when his arrogance leads him into trouble. Some stories highlight the value of cleverness and quick thinking, while others caution against being too cunning for your own good. Coyote's tricks are always entertaining, but they also leave the listener with something to think about, whether it's a moral lesson or a reflection on the unpredictability of life.

In conclusion, Coyote is one of the most complex and intriguing figures in Native American mythology. His clever tricks, whether they lead to success or disaster, teach important lessons about life, nature, and human behavior. Through his stories, we learn that intelligence and cunning can be powerful tools, but they must be used wisely. Coyote's actions remind us that life is full of surprises, and that even the best plans can have unintended consequences. His tales of trickery and mischief continue to captivate audiences, offering timeless insights into the human condition. Though he is a troublemaker, Coyote's cleverness, resilience, and unpredictable nature make him an unforgettable character in the rich tapestry of Native American lore.

Chapter 12: The Legend of Ganesha and His Elephant Head

The legend of Ganesha, the beloved elephant-headed god, is one of the most famous and cherished stories in Hindu mythology. Ganesha is known as the remover of obstacles, the god of wisdom, and the patron of arts and sciences. He is easily recognizable by his elephant head and large belly, and is often depicted holding various objects that symbolize his divine powers. His image is a source of comfort and inspiration for millions of people, as he is invoked at the beginning of new ventures, journeys, and ceremonies to ensure success and remove any difficulties that might arise. But how did Ganesha come to have the head of an elephant? The story of his birth and transformation into the elephant-headed deity is filled with deep meaning, magical events, and important lessons about loyalty, devotion, and the power of forgiveness.

The most widely known version of Ganesha's origin story begins with the goddess Parvati, the wife of Lord Shiva, one of the three most powerful gods in Hinduism. Parvati, like any other goddess, had immense power, but she was also depicted as loving, caring, and motherly. One day, while Lord Shiva was away meditating in the mountains, Parvati decided that she wanted a child to keep her company and bring her joy. Using her divine powers, Parvati took some turmeric paste (a substance commonly used by women for bathing in ancient times) from her own body and shaped it into the form of a boy. She then breathed life into this figure, creating a beautiful son. Parvati named her son Ganesha and loved him dearly. She raised him with affection, teaching him all that he needed to know, and he became her loyal companion.

Ganesha was devoted to his mother, and as he grew, Parvati entrusted him with more responsibilities. One day, Parvati wished to take a bath, and she asked Ganesha to stand guard outside her chambers, instructing him not to let anyone enter. Ganesha, being a dutiful son, agreed and stood at the door, determined to fulfill his mother's request. At that very moment, however, Lord Shiva returned home after his long meditation. He approached Parvati's chambers but was surprised to find a young boy he didn't recognize standing at the entrance.

Ganesha, not knowing who Shiva was, blocked his path and refused to let him enter. "My mother has told me not to let anyone pass," Ganesha declared firmly. Shiva, shocked that this boy would prevent him from entering his own home, demanded that Ganesha step aside. But Ganesha, loyal to his mother's wishes, stood his ground and refused. This angered Shiva, who was not used to being defied. He warned Ganesha to move, but Ganesha remained steadfast, determined to carry out his mother's instructions.

As tensions escalated, Shiva's anger got the better of him. He was known for his temper, and in a fit of rage, he unleashed his divine powers against Ganesha. The two fought fiercely, and Shiva, in his wrath, struck off Ganesha's head with his powerful trident. The lifeless body of Ganesha fell to the ground. Shiva's anger quickly subsided, but by then it was too late—Ganesha was gone.

When Parvati discovered what had happened, she was overwhelmed with grief and fury. She loved her son deeply, and the sight of his lifeless body filled her with unimaginable sorrow. In her anguish, Parvati demanded that Shiva restore their son to life immediately. She threatened to destroy the entire universe with her grief if Ganesha was not brought back. Realizing the gravity of the situation and regretting his impulsive actions, Shiva promised Parvati that he would bring their son back to life.

However, Shiva faced a problem—Ganesha's original head had been destroyed during the battle. He needed to find a replacement. Shiva sent his attendants, known as the Ganas, out into the world with instructions to find the head of the first living creature they came across and bring it back to him. The Ganas searched far and wide, and the first creature they encountered was a powerful elephant. They took the elephant's head and brought it back to Shiva.

With the elephant's head in hand, Shiva used his divine powers to place it on Ganesha's body. He then breathed life back into the boy, bringing Ganesha back from the dead. Parvati was overjoyed to see her son alive again, though he now had the head of an elephant. She embraced him lovingly, grateful for his return. From that moment on, Ganesha became known as the elephant-headed god, a figure who is both wise and powerful.

But the story doesn't end there. To make amends for his actions and to honor Ganesha, Shiva bestowed upon him a unique blessing. He declared that Ganesha would be the lord of new beginnings and the remover of obstacles. No undertaking, whether big or small, could begin without first seeking Ganesha's blessings. Shiva also made Ganesha the leader of his attendants, the Ganas, which is why Ganesha is sometimes referred to as "Ganapati," meaning the lord of the Ganas. In addition to these honors, Ganesha was also given dominion over wisdom, intellect, and learning, making him the patron god of scholars, artists, and anyone seeking knowledge.

The elephant head of Ganesha holds deep symbolic meaning. In Hindu culture, elephants are considered wise, strong, and gentle creatures. The large head of Ganesha represents wisdom and the ability to think big, while his large ears symbolize the importance of listening carefully to others. His small eyes are said to represent concentration and focus, and his trunk, which can pick up both heavy objects and delicate flowers, symbolizes adaptability and the ability to handle both the big and small challenges in life. Ganesha's broken tusk is also a symbol of sacrifice, as one legend says that he broke it off to write the epic Mahabharata, showing that wisdom often requires personal sacrifice.

Over time, Ganesha's popularity grew, and he became one of the most widely worshipped gods in Hinduism. His elephant head and rotund body make him instantly recognizable, and his image can be found in temples, homes, and festivals throughout India and around the world. He is often depicted with four arms, holding various objects that each have their own symbolic meaning. In one hand, he holds an axe, which represents the ability to cut through obstacles and negativity. In another hand, he holds a rope, which symbolizes pulling oneself closer to spiritual goals. In yet another hand, he holds a sweet, usually a modak, which represents the rewards of a disciplined life and the sweetness of the soul. His fourth hand is often shown in a gesture of blessing, reminding devotees that Ganesha is always there to help and protect them.

Another interesting aspect of Ganesha is his vehicle, the tiny mouse or rat known as Mushika. The contrast between the mighty Ganesha and his small vehicle is often seen as a reminder that even the smallest beings can overcome the greatest obstacles. The mouse, which is small and can sneak into the tiniest spaces, symbolizes the ability to navigate through the challenges of life and the power of the mind to overcome even the most difficult problems.

The legend of Ganesha and his elephant head is not only a story of love and devotion between a mother and her son, but also a tale of forgiveness, redemption, and the transformative power of divine grace. Shiva's regret for his rash actions and his efforts to restore Ganesha show that even gods can make mistakes and must find ways to right their wrongs. Parvati's fierce love for her son and her demand for justice reflect the power of a mother's devotion. And Ganesha's new form, with his elephant head and divine powers, symbolizes the idea that even after great loss or transformation, one can emerge stronger and wiser.

Through his cleverness, kindness, and ability to overcome challenges, Ganesha has become a beloved figure for people of all ages.

His image and his story remind us that wisdom, patience, and perseverance are the keys to success, and that obstacles, no matter how large, can always be removed with the right mindset and approach. Ganesha's presence at the beginning of ceremonies, journeys, and new ventures ensures that those who call upon him are protected and guided, making him a symbol of hope, good fortune, and wisdom.

In the end, the legend of Ganesha and his elephant head is a story that resonates across time and cultures. It teaches us important lessons about loyalty, forgiveness, and the importance of staying true to one's word, while also reminding us that wisdom often comes from the most unexpected places. Ganesha's playful, yet powerful, nature makes him a figure who is both approachable and revered, embodying the balance between strength and gentleness, intellect and emotion, and chaos and order. His stories continue to inspire, offering guidance and comfort to those who seek his blessings in their lives.

Chapter 13: The Aztec Creation Story of the Fifth Sun

The Aztec creation story of the Fifth Sun is one of the most fascinating and complex myths in Mesoamerican culture. It tells the tale of how the world was created and destroyed multiple times before the current age, known as the Fifth Sun, came into existence. This story reflects the Aztecs' understanding of the universe as a cyclical process of creation and destruction, where powerful gods played crucial roles in shaping the world and humanity. The myth is filled with drama, sacrifice, and divine struggles, highlighting the Aztecs' beliefs about the balance of forces in the universe and the importance of sacrifice to maintain cosmic order.

According to the Aztec creation myth, there were four previous worlds, or "suns," that were created and destroyed before the Fifth Sun, which is the age we live in today. Each of these worlds was ruled by a different god and had its own unique characteristics, but all of them ended in cataclysmic events that wiped out life and forced the gods to begin again. The cycle of destruction and rebirth reflected the Aztecs' belief that the universe required constant renewal through sacrifice and divine effort.

The story begins with the creation of the first sun, known as the Sun of Earth. This world was ruled by Tezcatlipoca, the powerful god of the night sky, sorcery, and change. Tezcatlipoca was one of the most influential gods in the Aztec pantheon, and his rule over the first world set the stage for the future cycles. In this world, the inhabitants were giants who lived in peace and prosperity. However, Tezcatlipoca's reign did not last forever. Quetzalcoatl, another powerful god and often considered Tezcatlipoca's rival, grew jealous of Tezcatlipoca's control over the world and decided to challenge him. Quetzalcoatl, who was the god of wind, knowledge, and creation, used his power to knock

Tezcatlipoca out of the sky, causing the first sun to fall and the world to be plunged into darkness.

Without the sun, the world was consumed by chaos, and the giants who lived in it were devoured by jaguars, creatures that symbolized Tezcatlipoca's wrath. The first sun, along with its people, was destroyed, and the gods were forced to create a new world. This was the end of the Sun of Earth, the first cycle of creation.

After the destruction of the first sun, the gods gathered again to create the second sun, known as the Sun of Wind. This time, the world was ruled by Quetzalcoatl, the god who had previously overthrown Tezcatlipoca. In this new world, humans were created, and everything seemed to be going well. But just like the first world, the second world was also destined for destruction. Tezcatlipoca, seeking revenge for his previous defeat, decided to bring an end to Quetzalcoatl's world. He transformed the people into monkeys and unleashed a great wind that swept across the land, tearing everything apart. The second sun was blown away by the wind, marking the end of the Sun of Wind and the second cycle of creation.

The gods, once again, had to start over. The third sun, known as the Sun of Fire, was ruled by the god Tlaloc, the god of rain and water. Tlaloc was responsible for bringing life-giving rain to the earth, and under his rule, the world flourished. But even this world could not escape its fate. Quetzalcoatl, who had grown dissatisfied with Tlaloc's rule, caused a great fire to consume the world. The fire scorched the earth, and the people who lived in this world were turned into birds. The third sun was destroyed by fire, bringing an end to the Sun of Fire.

The fourth sun, known as the Sun of Water, was ruled by Tlaloc's wife, the goddess Chalchiuhtlicue, who was the deity of rivers, lakes, and seas. Chalchiuhtlicue was a kind and nurturing goddess, and her world was filled with beauty and abundance. However, even this world was not meant to last. The gods, who had become increasingly frustrated with the failures of the previous suns, once again decided to destroy this world. This time, it was destroyed by a massive flood that covered the entire earth. The people of the fourth world were transformed into fish, and the sun was swallowed by the waters, bringing an end to the Sun of Water.

After the destruction of the fourth sun, the gods gathered in a place called Teotihuacan, which was one of the most sacred places in the Aztec world. They knew that they needed to create a new world, a Fifth Sun, but they also realized that this new world would require great sacrifice. The gods understood that the universe needed energy to keep the sun moving through the sky, and that energy could only be provided through the offering of divine blood.

Two gods stepped forward to sacrifice themselves to become the new sun: Tecciztecatl, a proud and wealthy god, and Nanahuatzin, a humble and sickly god. Tecciztecatl was covered in wealth and adorned with fine clothes, while Nanahuatzin was poor and covered in sores. Both gods were expected to throw themselves into a great fire to be transformed into the new sun, but when the moment came, Tecciztecatl hesitated. He was too afraid of the pain and the flames. Nanahuatzin, on the other hand, bravely threw himself into the fire without a second thought, and he was transformed into the Fifth Sun. Tecciztecatl, feeling ashamed, eventually followed Nanahuatzin and threw himself into the fire, but because he had hesitated, he became the moon instead of the sun. His light was dim and pale compared to the brilliance of Nanahuatzin's sun.

Though Nanahuatzin had become the new sun, the world was still dark because the sun was not moving through the sky. The gods realized that more sacrifice was needed to give the sun the strength to rise and set each day. In a dramatic act of self-sacrifice, the gods offered their own blood to empower the sun. This was the ultimate act of divine generosity and responsibility—the gods gave up part of themselves to ensure that the universe would continue to function. With their blood, the sun gained the energy it needed, and the Fifth Sun began to rise and set, bringing light and warmth to the world.

The Fifth Sun, the world we live in today, is the product of this incredible sacrifice. But the Aztecs believed that the survival of this world was not guaranteed. They believed that the gods needed constant offerings of blood and human sacrifice to keep the sun moving through the sky. Without these sacrifices, the sun would stop, and the world would come to an end, just like the previous four suns. This belief was at the core of Aztec religious practices, where human sacrifice played a central role. The Aztecs saw these sacrifices not as acts of cruelty, but as necessary offerings to maintain the balance of the universe and ensure the continuation of life.

The myth of the Fifth Sun is deeply symbolic, representing the Aztec worldview in which life, death, and rebirth are part of an endless cycle. The gods, despite their power, were not able to create a perfect world without sacrifice. Each of the previous suns represented different forces of nature—earth, wind, fire, and water—that had to be balanced to create a stable world. The Fifth Sun, however, required the ultimate sacrifice: the lives of the gods themselves. This act of self-sacrifice taught the Aztecs that even the most powerful beings must give of themselves for the greater good.

The story also reflects the Aztecs' deep connection to their environment and their dependence on the forces of nature. The destruction of the first four suns by natural disasters—jaguars, wind, fire, and flood—emphasized the idea that the world is fragile and constantly under threat from the elements. This fragility made the Aztecs acutely aware of the need to maintain balance in the universe through ritual and sacrifice.

In addition to its cosmic significance, the myth of the Fifth Sun also contains important lessons about courage and humility. Nanahuatzin, the humble and sickly god, was the one who had the courage to become the sun, while Tecciztecatl, the wealthy and proud god, hesitated. This teaches that greatness comes from selflessness and bravery, not from wealth or status. Nanahuatzin's willingness to sacrifice himself for the good of the universe is a powerful reminder of the importance of humility and service to others.

Today, the Aztec creation story of the Fifth Sun continues to captivate the imagination of people around the world. It offers a glimpse into the rich and complex worldview of the Aztec civilization, with its deep respect for the forces of nature, its belief in the cyclical nature of time, and its emphasis on sacrifice as a way to maintain the balance of the universe. The story reminds us that the world we live in is the product of great effort and sacrifice, and that we have a responsibility to honor and preserve the delicate balance that sustains life on earth.

Chapter 14: The Guardians of the Inca Andes

The Guardians of the Inca Andes are an important part of the ancient Incan belief system, representing the spirits and deities that protected the towering Andes Mountains and the people who lived within them. The Incas, who built one of the largest and most powerful empires in the Americas, believed that their world was filled with divine forces, each tied to specific places in nature. Among these, the guardians of the mountains, known as *apus*, held a special place in their hearts and minds.

The Incas viewed the Andes not just as a physical landscape but as a sacred space filled with life and power. The towering peaks of the mountains were seen as the homes of the *apus*, protective spirits who watched over the land, its people, and even the weather. These mighty deities were believed to control many aspects of daily life, from providing the rains necessary for crops to grow, to protecting the people from enemies, to ensuring the health and prosperity of the community. The Incas saw the mountains as living beings, and their guardians were deeply respected and honored in rituals and ceremonies.

Each mountain was believed to have its own *apu*, and these spiritual beings were seen as extremely powerful, sometimes even more so than the other deities in the Incan pantheon. The Incas believed that the *apus* were responsible for the well-being of the people who lived in the valleys and slopes below the mountains. They could bless the people with fertility, health, and protection, but they could also bring misfortune if they were not properly respected. The *apus* were not just spirits of the mountains themselves, but they also represented the forces of nature and the balance between the earth, sky, and water.

To honor the *apus*, the Incas performed various rituals and offerings. These were often conducted by priests or shamans, who would climb the steep slopes of the mountains to make their offerings at high altitudes, close to the sacred peaks. These offerings could include food, chicha (a traditional corn beer), coca leaves, and sometimes even animals, such as llamas. In rare cases, when the Incas believed that a particularly powerful event or blessing was needed, they would perform human sacrifices, offering the lives of young children to the *apus* in a practice called *capacocha*. These children were usually chosen for their beauty and purity, and the sacrifice was considered a great honor, as they were believed to join the gods in the afterlife.

One of the most important *apus* in Incan culture was Apu Ausangate, a guardian spirit associated with one of the highest and most sacred mountains in Peru. Ausangate, located near Cusco, was believed to control the waters that flowed from the glaciers, feeding the rivers and lakes that provided life to the surrounding valleys. The Inca believed that the rain, snow, and ice that fell on the Andes came from the breath of the *apus*, who controlled the weather and the seasons. As a result, the people would often pray to Ausangate for good harvests, fertility, and protection from drought or storms.

The Incas also believed that the *apus* were linked to the Sun God, Inti, who was the most important deity in the Inca pantheon. Inti was considered the father of the Inca emperors, and he played a central role in the Incan religion. The connection between the *apus* and Inti was strong, as the mountains reached towards the sky and the sun, bridging the gap between the earth and the heavens. In fact, the Inca emperor himself was often seen as a living representative of the *apus* and Inti, acting as a mediator between the gods and the people. The emperor's divine connection to the *apus* reinforced his authority and the sacredness of his rule.

The sacred nature of the *apus* extended beyond their role as guardians of the physical world. They were also believed to be protectors of the Incan ancestors. The Incas believed in *ayllus*, which were kinship groups or extended families that lived together and shared resources. Each *ayllu* had its own *apu* that watched over its members and ensured their prosperity. The people would offer prayers and sacrifices to their *apu* to seek guidance, protection, and success in their endeavors. The *apus* were seen as both spiritual and ancestral guardians, connecting the living with those who had passed on.

In addition to their protective roles, the *apus* were also associated with wisdom and knowledge. The Incas believed that the *apus* held ancient wisdom that could be accessed through prayer, meditation, and rituals. The priests and shamans who communicated with the *apus* were highly respected members of society, as they were seen as intermediaries between the human world and the divine realm. These spiritual leaders would often interpret the will of the *apus*, offering advice on when to plant crops, how to avoid disasters, and how to maintain harmony within the community.

The relationship between the Incas and the *apus* was one of deep reverence and reciprocity. The people depended on the *apus* for survival, and in return, they showed their gratitude through offerings and ceremonies. This sense of reciprocity was central to the Incan worldview, which emphasized the importance of maintaining balance and harmony in all aspects of life. The concept of *ayni*, or mutual exchange, was fundamental to Incan society, and it extended to their relationship with the natural world and the *apus*. By honoring the *apus*, the Incas believed that they were ensuring the continued flow of blessings and protection from the gods.

The *apus* were not only revered in life but also in death. When someone passed away, especially a member of the nobility, the Incas would often take the body to a sacred mountain to be buried near the summit. This practice was believed to bring the deceased closer to the gods and the *apus*, allowing their spirit to continue watching over their descendants. The mountains themselves were seen as gateways to the afterlife, where the souls of the dead could join the ranks of the *apus* and other divine beings.

The legacy of the *apus* continues to this day. In the Andean regions of Peru, Bolivia, Ecuador, and Chile, many indigenous communities still honor the *apus* with ceremonies and offerings, just as their ancestors did. These rituals, known as *pachamancas* or *apachetas*, are performed to ask for blessings, protection, and good fortune. The mountains remain sacred places, and people continue to climb to the high altitudes to make offerings of food, drink, and coca leaves to the *apus*. The belief in the guardianship of the *apus* is a living tradition that has endured for centuries, connecting modern-day Andean communities to their ancient Incan heritage.

In modern times, many people who visit the Andes are drawn to the mountains not only for their natural beauty but also for their spiritual significance. Travelers and pilgrims alike seek to connect with the powerful energy of the *apus*, hoping to gain insight, healing, or simply a sense of peace. The Andes Mountains, with their towering peaks and vast landscapes, continue to inspire awe and reverence, just as they did for the Incas.

The *apus* are more than just guardians of the mountains; they are guardians of the people, the land, and the very essence of life itself. They represent the interconnectedness of the natural world and the divine, and they remind us of the importance of respect, balance, and harmony in all things. Through their protection and guidance, the *apus* helped the Inca Empire thrive, and their legacy lives on in the hearts and minds of those who continue to honor them. The Guardians of the Inca Andes remain a powerful symbol of the enduring connection between humanity and the sacred forces of nature.

Chapter 15: The Celtic Story of the Salmon of Wisdom

The Celtic story of the Salmon of Wisdom is one of the most famous and cherished legends in Irish mythology. It weaves together the magical themes of knowledge, destiny, and transformation, and it has been passed down through generations, captivating the imagination of people both young and old. This myth is deeply rooted in the ancient Celtic reverence for nature and the belief that wisdom and power could be found in the natural world, particularly in animals, trees, and sacred places. The story of the Salmon of Wisdom not only tells of the quest for knowledge but also reveals the interconnectedness of all life, the importance of patience, and the idea that wisdom often comes when least expected.

According to the legend, long ago in ancient Ireland, there was a mystical fish known as the Salmon of Wisdom, or the Salmon of Knowledge. This fish was said to possess all the knowledge of the world, and whoever ate its flesh would instantly gain this wisdom. The salmon lived in a sacred pool called the Well of Wisdom, or sometimes referred to as the Well of Segais, which was located deep in the heart of a forest. The pool was surrounded by nine magical hazel trees, and it was said that these trees produced nuts that contained the knowledge of the universe. Whenever one of the hazel nuts fell into the pool, the salmon would eat it, and with every nut it consumed, the salmon became wiser and more powerful.

The Well of Wisdom and its magical salmon were hidden from ordinary people, and only a few, such as druids and poets, knew of its existence. Druids were highly respected figures in Celtic society, acting as priests, teachers, and keepers of sacred knowledge. They understood that wisdom was not something easily attained—it required patience, dedication, and, sometimes, the intervention of the divine. The legend of the Salmon of Wisdom reflects the druids' belief that true knowledge could not be forced or rushed; it had to come naturally, just as the salmon gained wisdom slowly by consuming the hazel nuts over time.

The most famous version of the story begins with a druid named Finegas (or Finn Éces), who had spent many years living by the River Boyne, studying its waters and the sacred pool in hopes of catching the elusive Salmon of Wisdom. Finegas was a wise old man who had dedicated his life to the pursuit of knowledge, and he knew that if he could catch and eat the salmon, he would be granted all the wisdom of the world. Day after day, Finegas sat by the river, watching and waiting for the salmon to appear. He fished tirelessly, but the salmon always remained just out of reach, as though it were testing his patience.

One day, a young boy named Fionn mac Cumhaill came to live with Finegas. Fionn, who would later become one of the greatest heroes in Irish mythology, was sent to Finegas to be taught the ways of wisdom and leadership. The boy was eager to learn and was a fast learner, always paying close attention to Finegas' teachings about the natural world, the gods, and the ancient stories of their people. Fionn was bright and curious, but he was still young and had much to learn about the deeper mysteries of life.

While Fionn studied with Finegas, the old druid continued his quest to catch the Salmon of Wisdom. Then, one fateful day, after many years of waiting, Finegas finally caught the salmon. He was overjoyed, knowing that his long quest for wisdom was about to come to an end. As he prepared to cook the salmon, he turned to Fionn and asked the young boy to watch the fish as it roasted over the fire. Finegas warned Fionn not to eat any part of the fish, as the wisdom it contained was meant for the druid alone.

Fionn dutifully tended to the fire, making sure the salmon cooked evenly. However, as he turned the fish on the spit, a drop of hot fish oil splattered onto his thumb. Instinctively, Fionn put his thumb in his mouth to cool the burn. In that moment, something incredible happened—Fionn felt a surge of knowledge and understanding flood his mind. Although he had only tasted a tiny bit of the salmon, it was enough to grant him the wisdom that Finegas had sought for so long.

When Finegas returned, he immediately noticed a change in Fionn. There was a new light in the boy's eyes, a sense of calm and understanding that had not been there before. Finegas asked Fionn if he had eaten any of the salmon, and the boy explained what had happened. The old druid realized that it was Fionn, not himself, who was destined to gain the wisdom of the salmon. Although Finegas had spent years in pursuit of the magical fish, the wisdom it contained was not meant for him. He graciously accepted this turn of fate, acknowledging that the boy was destined for greatness.

From that day forward, Fionn possessed the wisdom of the Salmon of Knowledge. It was said that whenever he needed to access this wisdom, all he had to do was place his thumb in his mouth, just as he had done when he burned it on the salmon. This newfound wisdom helped Fionn become the legendary leader of the Fianna, a group of elite warriors who defended Ireland from threats and maintained justice across the land. Fionn's wisdom guided him through many challenges, and he became known not only for his strength and bravery but also for his deep understanding of the world and his ability to lead with fairness and compassion.

The story of the Salmon of Wisdom is more than just a tale of magical fish and ancient druids; it carries deep meanings and lessons that have resonated with generations of people. One of the central themes of the story is the idea that true wisdom cannot be forced or rushed. Finegas, despite his years of study and dedication, could not make the salmon appear until the time was right. Even then, it was Fionn, the unassuming boy, who was destined to receive the wisdom. This teaches us that wisdom often comes in unexpected ways and that sometimes, we must be patient and let things unfold in their own time.

Another important lesson in the story is the concept of destiny. Despite Finegas' best efforts, he was not the one chosen to gain the wisdom of the salmon. Instead, it was Fionn, a young boy with a bright future, who was meant to inherit this knowledge. This reflects the Celtic belief in *fate* or *geis*, the idea that certain events and outcomes are preordained by the gods. No matter how hard we try to control our lives, some things are beyond our power, and we must trust that what is meant to be will come to pass.

The role of nature in the story is also significant. The salmon, the hazel trees, and the sacred pool are all symbols of the natural world, and they remind us that wisdom and knowledge are not separate from nature but are deeply connected to it. In ancient Celtic culture, the natural world was seen as a source of divine power and wisdom. The druids, in particular, believed that the land, animals, and plants held spiritual significance, and they often sought guidance and inspiration from the natural world. The salmon's connection to the hazel trees, which represented knowledge, further emphasizes the idea that wisdom comes from the earth itself.

Additionally, the relationship between Finegas and Fionn highlights the importance of mentorship and learning. Fionn's time with Finegas was a period of growth and education, where he absorbed the teachings of his mentor and prepared for his future role as a leader. The story reminds us that wisdom is often passed down from one generation to the next, through teaching, experience, and storytelling. Even though Finegas did not gain the wisdom of the salmon himself, his guidance and instruction were crucial in preparing Fionn to become the hero he was destined to be.

Finally, the story of the Salmon of Wisdom can be seen as a metaphor for the journey of life itself. Just as the salmon swims against the current to reach its destination, so too must we navigate the challenges and obstacles of life in our search for understanding and purpose. The salmon's journey mirrors our own quest for knowledge, growth, and fulfillment, and it reminds us that the path to wisdom is not always easy, but it is always worthwhile.

In conclusion, the Celtic story of the Salmon of Wisdom is a rich and enduring legend that speaks to the timeless themes of patience, destiny, and the interconnectedness of all life. It tells the tale of how a young boy, Fionn mac Cumhaill, gained the wisdom of the world through a simple act of fate and how that wisdom helped him become one of Ireland's greatest heroes. The story reminds us that true wisdom often comes when we least expect it and that the natural world is a source of deep knowledge and power. It is a tale that has captured the imagination of countless generations and continues to inspire those who seek to understand the mysteries of life.

Chapter 16: The Love Story of Odin and Frigg

The love story of Odin and Frigg is one of the most beautiful and enduring tales in Norse mythology. It speaks of love, loyalty, wisdom, and sacrifice, intertwined with the fates of gods and mortals alike. Odin, the All-Father and ruler of Asgard, and Frigg, the queen of the gods, shared a bond that was both powerful and complex, reflecting the deepest emotions and mysteries of life. Together, they stood at the center of the Norse pantheon, their love influencing the destinies of gods and humans alike.

Odin was the most powerful of all the gods, known for his wisdom, warlike prowess, and desire for knowledge. He ruled over Asgard, the realm of the gods, and was associated with many things, including battle, death, poetry, and magic. Odin was often portrayed as a mysterious figure, always searching for more knowledge, even sacrificing himself on the World Tree, Yggdrasil, to gain the secrets of the runes. His thirst for wisdom and power sometimes led him on dangerous quests, as he sought to understand the past, present, and future.

Frigg, on the other hand, was the goddess of love, marriage, motherhood, and destiny. She was known for her incredible wisdom, rivaling even that of Odin himself. Frigg was also associated with spinning and weaving, as it was said that she spun the threads of fate. This made her an important figure in the lives of both gods and mortals, as she had the power to influence the future. Despite her wisdom, Frigg was often portrayed as a more compassionate and nurturing figure than her husband, embodying the qualities of a caring mother and protector.

The relationship between Odin and Frigg was built on mutual respect and deep affection, but it was also shaped by the complexities of their roles as divine rulers. Odin, being the All-Father, had many responsibilities and often wandered through the Nine Realms in search of wisdom and adventure. This meant that he was frequently absent from Asgard, leaving Frigg to govern in his place. Frigg, with her deep wisdom and understanding, was more than capable of ruling in Odin's stead, but she missed her husband's presence, and this distance between them was one of the challenges they faced in their relationship.

Despite Odin's wanderings, his love for Frigg remained constant. Frigg, too, was deeply devoted to her husband, even though she sometimes foresaw difficult or tragic events in the future, especially those that would affect their family. One of the most poignant aspects of their relationship was Frigg's ability to see the future but her inability to change it. This was a burden she carried, knowing the fates of her loved ones but being powerless to alter their destinies.

One of the most tragic stories connected to Odin and Frigg is the death of their son, Balder. Balder was the god of light, joy, and beauty, beloved by all the gods and mortals alike. His death was foretold in a dream, and when Frigg learned of it, she was overcome with grief. Determined to protect her son, Frigg went to every corner of the world, extracting promises from all living things—plants, animals, and even stones—that they would not harm Balder. She overlooked only one thing: mistletoe, thinking it too small and insignificant to be dangerous.

Loki, the trickster god, discovered this oversight and crafted a dart made from mistletoe. During a game where the gods playfully threw weapons at Balder, knowing he was invulnerable, Loki gave the mistletoe dart to Balder's blind brother, Höðr, who unknowingly threw it at Balder. The dart struck Balder and killed him, plunging the gods into mourning. Odin and Frigg were devastated by the loss of their beloved son, and despite their immense power, there was nothing they could do to bring him back from Hel, the realm of the dead.

Frigg's sorrow over Balder's death is one of the most heartbreaking aspects of Norse mythology. She had tried so hard to protect her son, using her wisdom and her love, but in the end, fate was stronger. This story highlights the theme of fate, which runs through many Norse myths. Even the gods were subject to the forces of destiny, and Frigg, despite her great power, could not prevent the tragedy she had foreseen.

Odin, too, was deeply affected by Balder's death. As the All-Father, he was known for being somewhat distant and inscrutable, often making difficult decisions that affected the fates of many. However, Balder's death showed a more vulnerable side of Odin. He mourned his son deeply and took actions to try to avenge him and prevent further tragedy, but like Frigg, he was bound by the inescapable web of fate.

The love between Odin and Frigg was tested by this great loss, but it did not break. Instead, their bond seemed to grow stronger in the face of adversity. Frigg, though consumed by grief, continued to fulfill her duties as queen of the gods, and Odin, despite his sorrow, remained committed to his responsibilities as the ruler of Asgard. Their love was not one of constant joy and harmony, but rather a deep and enduring connection that withstood the trials of time, destiny, and loss.

Beyond the tragic story of Balder, there are many other tales that speak to the unique and powerful relationship between Odin and Frigg. One such story is the competition between Odin and Frigg over which of two noble families would win a race. Odin supported one family, while Frigg favored the other. Using her cunning, Frigg tricked Odin by sending her servant to sabotage the race, ensuring that her chosen family would win. When Odin discovered the trick, he was not angry but rather amused by his wife's cleverness. This story illustrates the playful and sometimes competitive dynamic between the two, as well as the respect Odin had for Frigg's intelligence.

Odin and Frigg's love also extended beyond their own personal relationship, as they were both deeply involved in the affairs of the gods and mortals. Odin, as a god of war, often sought to influence battles and conflicts, while Frigg, as a goddess of fertility and motherhood, was more concerned with the well-being of families and communities. Together, they balanced each other's strengths and weaknesses, creating a harmonious partnership that helped maintain order in the cosmos.

Frigg's role as a mother extended beyond her own children. She was seen as a protector of families, and many Norse women prayed to her for guidance and blessings in matters of childbirth, marriage, and home life. Frigg's nurturing nature made her a beloved goddess among the Norse people, especially women, who saw her as a symbol of strength, wisdom, and compassion. Her love for Odin, though central to her story, was just one aspect of her powerful presence in Norse mythology.

Odin's love for Frigg was equally profound. Despite his many quests for knowledge and power, he always returned to her. Their relationship was one of mutual respect, where each recognized the other's strengths and contributions. Odin's respect for Frigg's wisdom was especially evident in the way he often sought her counsel on important matters. While he was known for his insatiable desire for knowledge, he understood that Frigg's wisdom, rooted in her deep understanding of fate and the natural world, was just as valuable as the secrets he gained through his own quests.

Their love also represented the union of different aspects of the cosmos—Odin, associated with the sky, storms, and the more warlike, unpredictable forces of nature, and Frigg, connected to the earth, fertility, and the steady rhythms of life and death. Together, they embodied the balance of chaos and order, war and peace, knowledge and intuition, making them a powerful and complementary pair.

As time passed, the love story of Odin and Frigg became one of the most enduring aspects of Norse mythology, symbolizing the strength of partnership and the resilience of love in the face of hardship. Even after the fall of the gods during Ragnarok, the end of the world in Norse mythology, the memory of their love survived in the stories told by the people. Their relationship, full of both joy and sorrow, reflected the complexities of life and the idea that love is not always easy, but it is always worth fighting for.

In conclusion, the love story of Odin and Frigg is a tale of deep affection, respect, and resilience. Their relationship was built on mutual understanding, and despite the challenges they faced—such as the loss of their son, Balder, and the burdens of their divine responsibilities—they remained devoted to one another. Odin, the All-Father, and Frigg, the wise and compassionate queen of the gods, were not only partners in love but also in leadership, each contributing to the balance of the cosmos. Their story continues to inspire, reminding us that love, even among the gods, is a powerful force that can endure through the most difficult trials.

Chapter 17: The Mystical Journey of the Rainbow Serpent

The mystical journey of the Rainbow Serpent is one of the most ancient and revered stories in the mythology of the Aboriginal people of Australia. This myth is deeply rooted in their culture and has been passed down through countless generations, explaining the creation of the land, the rivers, the mountains, and the animals. The Rainbow Serpent is a powerful and mysterious being that holds great significance for the Aboriginal people, representing both creation and destruction, life and death. This epic journey is not just a story of one serpent, but of the birth of the world itself, a world filled with life, wonder, and magic.

Long ago, before the world looked anything like it does today, the land was flat, dry, and barren. There were no trees, no rivers, no hills—just a vast, empty plain under the scorching sun. The creatures that would one day fill the land had not yet been created, and the world lay still in silence. In this quiet, desolate place, the Rainbow Serpent slumbered beneath the earth, coiled in the dark underground. She was a massive being, with a long, colorful body that shimmered like the colors of a rainbow, even in the darkness. The serpent had been sleeping for ages, waiting for the right time to awaken and begin her journey.

As the story goes, the Rainbow Serpent awoke from her deep slumber when she sensed that it was time to create the world as we know it. She uncoiled her enormous body, stretching it out through the land, and as she moved, she began to shape the earth. With her writhing movements, she created the mountains, valleys, and hills, pushing the ground upward and carving out deep crevices. Her path became the rivers and waterways that would soon flow with life. The rivers wound and twisted just like the serpent herself, and their waters shimmered with the colors of the Rainbow Serpent's body.

As she journeyed across the land, the Rainbow Serpent left behind her a trail of life. Wherever she went, she created new features of the landscape, bringing beauty and diversity to the earth. The once-barren plains were now filled with tall trees, flowering plants, and winding rivers. The Serpent's power was so immense that even the sky responded to her presence. Storms rolled across the horizon, and rain began to fall, filling the rivers and lakes with fresh water. The land was no longer dry and empty; it was alive and flourishing, thanks to the Rainbow Serpent's work.

But the Rainbow Serpent's journey did not end there. As she traveled, she encountered other beings, the ancestors of the Aboriginal people, who were also beginning to awaken. These ancestral spirits, who took the form of animals, plants, and elements, had been asleep like the Rainbow Serpent, waiting for the right moment to come alive and begin their roles in shaping the world. The Rainbow Serpent called out to them, awakening them from their deep sleep, and together, they began to fill the world with more life.

The animals, birds, and insects sprang forth from the earth, each created by the ancestors with the help of the Rainbow Serpent. Kangaroos bounded across the newly formed plains, birds took to the skies, and fish swam in the rivers. The trees provided shelter for the animals, and the rivers gave them water to drink. The Rainbow Serpent had given them a home, a place to live and thrive, and now the earth was teeming with life.

As the animals spread across the land, the Rainbow Serpent continued her journey. She visited every corner of the land, ensuring that all creatures had a place to live. But with her great power also came great responsibility. The Rainbow Serpent was not only a creator but also a guardian of the land and its creatures. She watched over them, making sure that they respected the earth and each other. The Rainbow Serpent's journey was not just about creating life, but about maintaining balance in the world.

However, the Rainbow Serpent also had a more fearsome side. While she was a creator, she could also bring destruction if the balance was disturbed. If the animals or the people disrespected the land, did not take care of it, or fought amongst themselves, the Rainbow Serpent would become angry. She could unleash storms, floods, and droughts, reminding everyone of her immense power. The Aboriginal people believed that the Rainbow Serpent had to be honored and respected because, just as she had created the land and all its creatures, she could also destroy them.

One of the most important lessons that the Rainbow Serpent taught the Aboriginal people was the importance of harmony and respect for the earth. The land was a gift, and it was their responsibility to care for it, just as the Rainbow Serpent had done during her journey. The Rainbow Serpent's story is deeply intertwined with Aboriginal law and culture, teaching people how to live in balance with nature, how to respect the land, the animals, and each other.

As the Rainbow Serpent continued her journey, she became a symbol of life itself, representing the cycles of birth, death, and rebirth. Just as the serpent sheds its skin, so too did the earth go through cycles of change, renewal, and transformation. The Rainbow Serpent's journey was never truly over because the earth and its creatures were always evolving, always growing. In many ways, the Rainbow Serpent's story is a metaphor for the natural world—the rivers that continue to flow, the seasons that change, the storms that come and go.

In some versions of the story, the Rainbow Serpent eventually returns to the earth, burrowing back into the ground where she once slept. She does this to rest and regain her strength, waiting for the time when she will be needed again to restore balance to the world. Even while she sleeps, her presence is still felt. When the rainbow appears in the sky after a rainstorm, the Aboriginal people believe it is the Rainbow Serpent stretching across the heavens, watching over the land and reminding everyone of her power and her journey.

The Rainbow Serpent's connection to water is one of the most important aspects of her myth. Water is life-giving, and in many parts of Australia, where the land can be dry and arid, water is precious. The rivers and lakes created by the Rainbow Serpent are essential to the survival of the people and animals that live there. The Rainbow Serpent is often associated with rain, rivers, and waterfalls, all of which bring life to the land. Without water, the land would return to the dry, barren state it was in before the Rainbow Serpent's journey began.

The Rainbow Serpent also plays a role in many Aboriginal ceremonies and rituals. These ceremonies are held to honor the Rainbow Serpent, to ask for her blessings, and to ensure that the land continues to thrive. During these ceremonies, stories of the Rainbow Serpent's journey are retold, passing down the knowledge and wisdom of the ancestors to the next generation. The Rainbow Serpent is more than just a myth—she is a living symbol of the connection between the people, the land, and the spirits of their ancestors.

In the end, the mystical journey of the Rainbow Serpent is a story of creation, balance, and the deep connection between all living things. It is a tale that teaches us about the importance of respecting the earth and living in harmony with nature. The Rainbow Serpent's journey shaped the world we know today, bringing life to the land and the creatures that inhabit it. But her journey also continues, as her presence is felt in the rivers, the rainbows, and the storms, reminding us of the power and beauty of the natural world.

For the Aboriginal people of Australia, the Rainbow Serpent is more than just a figure from mythology. She is a protector, a creator, and a guide, showing them the way to live in harmony with the land and with each other. Her story is a reflection of their deep connection to the earth, and her journey is a reminder of the cycles of life that continue to shape the world around us. The Rainbow Serpent's journey is one of the most profound and sacred stories in Aboriginal culture, a story that continues to inspire and teach to this day.

Chapter 18: The Russian Baba Yaga and Her Magical Hut

The story of Baba Yaga is one of the most mysterious and captivating legends in Russian folklore. Baba Yaga is a witch, but not just any witch—she is one of the most complex figures in mythology, feared by many yet also sought after for her wisdom and magical powers. Her legend has been told and retold across generations, and her presence looms large in the minds of those who grow up hearing tales of her strange powers, her odd appearance, and, perhaps most intriguingly, her magical hut. Baba Yaga's magical hut, which stands on chicken legs, is just as famous as the witch herself. Together, they form the core of stories filled with danger, adventure, mystery, and even the possibility of transformation.

Baba Yaga is often described as an old, crone-like woman with wild, tangled hair, sharp, iron teeth, and long, bony fingers. She has a crooked nose and rides around in a mortar, using a pestle to guide her way through the air or across the ground. She lives deep in the forest, far away from towns and villages, and her presence is usually a sign of great danger or a test that a hero must face. Although she may seem terrifying, Baba Yaga is not purely evil. She can be helpful to those who are brave and respectful, but for those who are foolish or rude, she is a formidable and unforgiving force.

One of the most remarkable features of Baba Yaga's legend is her magical hut, which is unlike any other house in folklore. Baba Yaga's hut does not sit still on the ground like normal houses. Instead, it stands on gigantic chicken legs, capable of moving around whenever Baba Yaga wishes. The house itself seems to have a mind of its own, moving through the forest to evade unwanted visitors or to carry out Baba Yaga's commands. The hut is said to spin around and around, and it only stops when the right spell or command is given. In many stories, when a hero or visitor approaches the hut, they must call out, "Turn your back to the forest, your front to me!" before the house will settle down and allow them to enter.

Inside, the hut is just as strange as the outside. It is often depicted as cluttered and dark, filled with strange objects, potions, and herbs. Some versions of the story describe the hut as being much larger on the inside than it appears on the outside, almost like a magical maze filled with surprises. The air inside the hut is thick with the smell of herbs and smoke from Baba Yaga's cauldron, where she is often brewing strange potions or preparing food. Skulls and bones might be seen hanging from the roof or strewn about the ground, adding to the spooky atmosphere.

Despite its eerie appearance, Baba Yaga's hut is also a place of great power. Those who seek Baba Yaga's help often come to the hut, hoping to gain her wisdom or magical assistance. However, approaching Baba Yaga is not easy. She is known to test those who come to her, often setting impossible tasks or asking riddles. Only those who are brave, clever, and respectful can hope to gain her favor. In some stories, heroes who succeed in Baba Yaga's tasks are rewarded with magical gifts, guidance, or the knowledge they need to complete their quests. In others, those who fail are met with a much darker fate.

One of the most famous tales involving Baba Yaga is the story of Vasilisa the Beautiful. In this story, a young girl named Vasilisa is sent by her wicked stepmother to seek fire from Baba Yaga. Vasilisa's stepmother hopes that Baba Yaga will kill her, but with the help of a magical doll given to her by her deceased mother, Vasilisa is able to survive her encounter with the witch. When Vasilisa reaches Baba Yaga's hut, she bravely recites the magic words to make the hut stop spinning. Baba Yaga demands that Vasilisa complete a series of impossible tasks, such as sorting out a huge pile of grains and cleaning the house from top to bottom. With the help of her doll, Vasilisa completes all the tasks, impressing Baba Yaga. Although Baba Yaga is fearsome and unpredictable, she keeps her word and gives Vasilisa the fire she needs. However, the fire is not ordinary—it is a glowing skull on a stick, and when Vasilisa returns home with it, the fire destroys her wicked stepmother and stepsisters, freeing Vasilisa from their cruelty.

In many ways, Baba Yaga's relationship with those who visit her is a reflection of their own character. If a person approaches her with respect and humility, she might help them. But if they come with arrogance or ill intentions, they are likely to face her wrath. Baba Yaga's hut is a symbol of her unpredictable nature. Just like the hut's chicken legs, which can lift the house and move it wherever it pleases, Baba Yaga is not bound by the rules of ordinary humans. She operates according to her own strange, magical logic, and it is up to those who encounter her to navigate that world wisely.

In some interpretations, Baba Yaga is seen as a guardian of the boundary between the living and the dead. Her hut is often surrounded by a fence made of bones, with skulls perched on top, their eyes glowing with an eerie light. This imagery suggests that Baba Yaga has power over life and death, and that those who enter her domain are stepping into a place where the normal rules of the world no longer apply. Some believe that Baba Yaga's magical hut serves as a gateway to the underworld, a place where the souls of the dead pass through on their journey to the afterlife.

Interestingly, despite her fearsome reputation, Baba Yaga is not always portrayed as a villain. In some stories, she is a neutral figure or even a helper to the hero. Her role in Russian folklore is complex, and she can be both a force of destruction and a source of wisdom. This dual nature makes Baba Yaga a unique character in mythology. She is neither purely good nor purely evil; she is a wild, untamable force of nature, reflecting the balance between life, death, and the natural world.

The magical hut of Baba Yaga is not just a place of danger; it is also a place of transformation. Heroes who enter the hut often leave changed, having gained new knowledge, strength, or understanding.

The hut, with its spinning walls and mysterious interior, represents the challenges that heroes must face in order to grow and evolve. It is a place where the boundaries between the known and the unknown blur, where the familiar world gives way to the strange and the magical. Those who are brave enough to step into the hut must be prepared to face their fears and prove their worth.

Baba Yaga and her magical hut have left a lasting impression on Russian folklore and beyond. Over time, Baba Yaga has become a symbol of the wild, untamed power of nature and the mysterious forces that lie just beyond the edges of the human world. Her hut, with its chicken legs and bone fence, is a reminder that magic and mystery are always just a step away, waiting to challenge or guide those who dare to seek them out.

The legend of Baba Yaga teaches us that not everything in the world is simple or straightforward. Some challenges require cunning and bravery to overcome, and sometimes, those who seem the most dangerous can also offer the greatest rewards. Baba Yaga's magical hut is a place where anything can happen, where the ordinary rules of the world do not apply. It is a place of magic, danger, and transformation—a place where heroes are tested and where the brave can find the strength to complete their journey.

Chapter 19: The Mayan Twins' Underworld Challenge

The story of the Mayan Twins, Hunahpu and Xbalanque, and their daring journey into the Underworld is one of the most thrilling and complex tales in Mayan mythology. This ancient legend is part of the *Popol Vuh*, a sacred book of the Maya that contains stories about their gods, heroes, and the creation of the world. The story of the Mayan Twins is not only an adventure filled with danger, clever tricks, and intense challenges, but it also represents the eternal struggle between light and darkness, life and death. It's a tale of bravery and wit, where two brothers use their intelligence and courage to face the terrifying lords of the Underworld, Xibalba, and come out victorious.

The journey begins long before the Twins, with the story of their father and uncle, who were also twins. Their names were Hun Hunahpu and Vucub Hunahpu. These two were exceptional ballplayers, known far and wide for their skill and strength. The ballgame was a sacred sport for the Maya, a game that symbolized the struggle between life and death. However, Hun Hunahpu and Vucub Hunahpu made a grave mistake—they were too loud when they played. Their constant noise and laughter disturbed the lords of the Underworld, the dark and fearsome rulers of Xibalba, who were angered by the disruption.

The lords of Xibalba, led by One Death and Seven Death, decided to put an end to the brothers' merriment. They sent messengers to summon Hun Hunahpu and Vucub Hunahpu to Xibalba. The brothers accepted the challenge, unaware of the deadly tricks awaiting them. When they arrived, the lords of the Underworld tricked and humiliated them, leading them through dangerous traps and tests. In the end, the brothers were defeated and killed. Their bodies were buried, and Hun Hunahpu's head was hung in a calabash tree as a warning to all who would dare challenge the lords of Xibalba.

But this was not the end. One day, a beautiful maiden named Xquic, the daughter of one of the lords of Xibalba, came to the tree. When she saw Hun Hunahpu's head, it spoke to her! Entranced by his voice, she reached out, and in a strange and magical way, the head spat into her hand. This spit contained the seed of life, and Xquic miraculously became pregnant. Furious, her father wanted to punish her, but Xquic managed to escape to the world above. There, she gave birth to twin boys—Hunahpu and Xbalanque.

From the moment they were born, the twins were no ordinary children. They were strong, clever, and daring, much like their father and uncle had been. As they grew up, they loved to play ball just like their father. But they did not know who their father was or what had happened to him. They played the game in secret, but like their father and uncle before them, they made a lot of noise. The echoes of their ballgame traveled far, reaching the ears of the lords of Xibalba once again. The lords, still holding a grudge, sent messengers to summon the young twins to the Underworld, just as they had done with their father and uncle.

This time, however, things would be different. Hunahpu and Xbalanque were not just skilled players; they were also wise and clever. They knew that the lords of Xibalba were full of trickery, so they prepared themselves. When they received the summons, they didn't go straight to Xibalba. Instead, they sent a mosquito ahead to spy on the lords. The mosquito buzzed around and bit each of the lords in turn, causing them to shout out their names. With this information, the Twins learned the true names of each of the Underworld rulers, a crucial advantage that would help them during their journey.

When Hunahpu and Xbalanque finally descended into Xibalba, they greeted each lord by name. This surprised the rulers, who were used to strangers being too afraid or confused to know who they were.

Realizing that the Twins were no ordinary visitors, the lords of Xibalba knew they had to be cunning. They began by leading the brothers through a series of deadly tests, designed to break their spirits and end their lives, just as they had done to their father and uncle.

The first test was the House of Darkness, a pitch-black room where the Twins were given a single torch and a cigar. The lords commanded that the torch and cigar must last the whole night, burning brightly until morning. The Twins knew that this was a trick—the torch and cigar would soon burn out, and they would be executed. But Hunahpu and Xbalanque were too clever for the lords of Xibalba. Instead of using the torch and cigar, they placed bright fireflies on the torch and a red feather on the cigar, making it appear as if both were still burning. When morning came, the lords were furious, but the Twins had passed the test.

Next, they were sent to the House of Knives, where razor-sharp blades flew through the air, slicing and dicing anything that moved. The Twins remained calm and used their magic to command the blades to stop. The knives froze in mid-air, allowing them to pass safely through the deadly house. Test after test, Hunahpu and Xbalanque outsmarted the lords of Xibalba. They faced the House of Cold, where icy winds howled through the chamber, threatening to freeze them solid. Using their wits, the Twins survived each challenge, outsmarting traps and turning the lords' tricks against them.

But the lords of Xibalba were not done yet. They sent the Twins to the House of Jaguars, where fierce, hungry jaguars waited to tear them apart. Instead of running or fighting, the Twins tossed bones to the jaguars, keeping them distracted until morning. Every challenge the lords threw at them, the Twins met with bravery and intelligence. Even in the terrifying House of Fire, where flames leaped up to the ceiling, the Twins found a way to survive without being burned.

Finally, the lords decided to use their most powerful weapon: the ballgame itself. They challenged the Twins to a match, hoping to defeat them and claim victory. But the Twins were masters of the game, just like their father and uncle had been. They played skillfully, dodging every trick and trap the lords tried to set. When the lords tried to cheat by using a deadly ball made of blades, Hunahpu and Xbalanque quickly realized what was happening and swapped the dangerous ball for a harmless one.

The Twins' victory over the lords of Xibalba was not just physical but also symbolic. Through their cleverness, they turned the tables on the lords, showing that light could overcome darkness and life could defeat death. In a final act of defiance, Hunahpu and Xbalanque allowed themselves to be killed by the lords—but this was part of their plan. After their execution, their bodies were thrown into the river, where they transformed into fish. Later, they rose again, shining like the sun and moon.

The Twins' resurrection marked the ultimate defeat of Xibalba. The lords, who had once been powerful and feared, were now powerless against the light and life that the Twins represented. Hunahpu and Xbalanque ascended to the sky, becoming the Sun and the Moon, symbols of life and renewal for the Maya people. Their journey into the Underworld, filled with challenges and danger, was not just about revenge or proving their strength—it was about restoring balance to the world, conquering death, and bringing hope to the people above.

The tale of the Mayan Twins' Underworld challenge is a story of courage, intelligence, and the triumph of life over darkness. It teaches that with wit and determination, even the greatest obstacles can be overcome. The legacy of Hunahpu and Xbalanque lives on, reminding us that light will always find a way to shine, even in the deepest, darkest places.

Chapter 20: The Dragon and the Pearl

In Vietnamese mythology, one of the most enchanting and symbolic tales is the story of the Dragon and the Pearl. This myth is rich with meaning, representing the connection between the natural world, the heavens, and the Vietnamese people. Dragons hold a special place in Vietnamese culture, and unlike the fire-breathing dragons of Western mythology, the dragons of Vietnam are benevolent and protective. They are seen as guardians of the land, water, and sky, with the power to control the rain, rivers, and seas. They bring prosperity, abundance, and life to the people. The story of the Dragon and the Pearl is not only a tale of mythical creatures but also a reflection of the deep respect the Vietnamese have for nature and the harmonious balance between all living things.

In the beginning, there was a great Dragon King who ruled over the seas and rivers. His domain was vast, stretching across the watery expanses of the world. The Dragon King was wise and powerful, and he was deeply respected by all creatures of the land and sea. He lived in an underwater palace made of shimmering pearls and precious gems, a place where the water was clear as crystal, and the fish swam freely through the sparkling currents. The Dragon King had many children, known as the Dragon Princes, who would one day rule over different parts of the land and water, ensuring the balance of nature was maintained.

The most prized possession of the Dragon King was a magical pearl, known as the *Ngọc*, or the "Pearl of Wisdom." This pearl was no ordinary gem—it glowed with an otherworldly light, radiating wisdom, peace, and power. The pearl had the ability to calm storms, bring rain to drought-stricken lands, and control the ebb and flow of the tides. It was said that whoever possessed the pearl could understand the secrets of the universe and gain incredible wisdom. The pearl represented the harmony between the heavens and the earth, between nature and humanity.

However, the pearl was not easily obtained or controlled. It was fiercely guarded by the Dragon King, who knew that if it fell into the wrong hands, it could bring chaos and destruction. Many creatures, both mortal and immortal, desired the pearl for its power. Legends speak of jealous demons, greedy rulers, and even other dragons who sought to steal the pearl from the Dragon King. But the King was always vigilant, keeping the pearl hidden deep within his palace, far from the reach of those with ill intentions.

One day, the Dragon King's youngest son, a curious and adventurous Dragon Prince, heard the stories of the magical pearl and became fascinated by its powers. Though he had never seen it with his own eyes, he longed to possess the pearl and understand its secrets. The Dragon Prince was brave and kind-hearted, but he was also impatient and headstrong, traits that would soon lead him into danger.

The Dragon Prince approached his father, asking to see the pearl and learn its wisdom. The Dragon King, knowing his son's nature, warned him of the pearl's immense power and the responsibility that came with it. He told his son that the pearl was not something to be taken lightly, and that only those who had mastered patience, humility, and understanding could hope to wield its power. The Dragon Prince, however, was determined. He believed that he could handle the pearl's magic and that he was ready for the challenge.

After much pleading, the Dragon King reluctantly agreed to show his son the pearl. He took the Dragon Prince to the deepest part of the palace, where the pearl rested on a pedestal of coral, glowing softly in the dim light. The sight of the pearl took the Dragon Prince's breath away. Its radiance filled the room with a warm, golden light, and the Prince could feel its power pulsing through the water, as if the pearl were alive.

The Dragon King told his son that the pearl could only be touched by those with pure hearts and clear minds. He warned the Dragon Prince once more, telling him that if he was not ready, the pearl's magic could overwhelm him. But the Dragon Prince, eager to prove himself, reached out and grasped the pearl. For a moment, everything was still. The water around him seemed to hum with energy, and the Dragon Prince felt as if he could hear the heartbeat of the earth itself. But then, something went wrong. The pearl's light grew brighter and hotter, and the Dragon Prince realized too late that he was not in control.

The pearl's magic surged through the Dragon Prince, filling him with knowledge and power beyond his understanding. Overwhelmed, the Dragon Prince lost his grip, and the pearl slipped from his hands. It fell from the pedestal and rolled out of the palace, carried by the currents of the sea. The Dragon Prince, horrified by what he had done, chased after it, but the pearl was swept away by the powerful ocean tides. It was lost to the depths of the sea.

The loss of the pearl was a great tragedy. Without the pearl's magic, the balance of nature began to unravel. Storms raged across the land, and the rivers swelled, flooding the fields and villages. The people, who relied on the gentle rains and calm seas brought by the Dragon King's pearl, now faced disaster. Crops failed, and famine spread across the land. The Dragon King was heartbroken by the loss of the pearl, but he did not blame his son. Instead, he told the Dragon Prince that it was now his responsibility to find the pearl and restore balance to the world.

Determined to make things right, the Dragon Prince set out on a perilous journey to recover the pearl. He traveled across the seas and rivers, through dark caves and over towering mountains, searching for any sign of the lost treasure. Along the way, he encountered many challenges—monstrous creatures, treacherous landscapes, and powerful sorcerers who also sought the pearl for themselves. But the Dragon Prince was brave and resilient, never giving up hope.

In one version of the story, the Dragon Prince meets a wise old turtle who knows the location of the pearl. The turtle tells the Prince that the pearl has been hidden by a giant serpent, a creature of darkness who seeks to use the pearl's power for evil. The serpent has taken the pearl to its lair, deep in the heart of a distant mountain. To retrieve the pearl, the Dragon Prince must face the serpent in battle and prove that he is worthy of the pearl's power.

The Dragon Prince, knowing the gravity of the task ahead, prepares himself for the final confrontation. He journeys to the mountain and finds the serpent's lair, a dark and forbidding cave filled with bones and treasures stolen from across the land. There, coiled around the pearl, is the giant serpent, its eyes glowing with malice. The serpent taunts the Dragon Prince, telling him that he is not strong enough to take back the pearl. But the Dragon Prince, remembering his father's teachings, knows that strength alone is not enough. He must use his mind and heart as well.

In the battle that follows, the Dragon Prince outsmarts the serpent, using his agility and wit to avoid the serpent's deadly strikes. With one final move, he manages to wrest the pearl from the serpent's grasp. As soon as he touches the pearl again, its light returns, filling the cave with warmth and dispelling the darkness. The serpent, unable to withstand the pearl's power, is vanquished, and the Dragon Prince emerges victorious.

With the pearl in hand, the Dragon Prince returns to his father's palace. The Dragon King, proud of his son's bravery and growth, welcomes him back. The pearl is restored to its rightful place, and with it, the balance of nature is also restored. The storms cease, the rivers return to their gentle flow, and the land is once again blessed with rain and abundance. The Dragon Prince, having learned the importance of patience, wisdom, and responsibility, becomes a great leader, ensuring that the pearl's power is used for the good of all.

The story of the Dragon and the Pearl is not just a tale of adventure; it is a lesson about the relationship between power and wisdom. The pearl, with its magical abilities, represents the knowledge and balance that must be handled with care. The Dragon Prince's journey is a metaphor for the growth and maturity that comes with understanding the responsibilities of power. It is a story that teaches the value of patience, humility, and the courage to face one's mistakes and make amends.

In Vietnamese culture, the dragon is a symbol of prosperity, strength, and protection. The story of the Dragon and the Pearl reflects these values, showing how the dragon's power can be used to maintain harmony and balance in the world. The pearl, with its connection to wisdom and the natural world, is a reminder that true power comes not from domination, but from understanding and respect for the forces of nature.

This myth has been passed down through generations, reminding the Vietnamese people of their connection to the land, water, and sky. It is a story that continues to inspire, teaching that even in times of darkness and difficulty, there is always a way to restore balance and find the light once again.

Epilogue

Our journey through the world's oldest stories has come to an end, but the magic of these myths is far from over. As you close this book, remember that these tales are not just stories from the past—they live on in the cultures, beliefs, and imaginations of people around the world. Each myth carries a piece of history, a glimpse into how people once saw the universe and their place within it.

These myths have taught us about courage, kindness, cleverness, and sometimes even the consequences of our mistakes. Whether it was Anansi the trickster weaving his webs, Maui pulling up islands from the ocean, or Odin sharing his wisdom, each story had something to share with us—something about the wonders of the world or the human heart.

Mythology reminds us that we are all connected, no matter where we come from. Different cultures may have different gods and heroes, but we all share a common desire to understand the world and to celebrate its mysteries. Myths are a part of our collective human story, passed down from our ancestors to us, and now to you.

Now, it's your turn to carry these stories forward. Tell them to your friends, share them with your family, or even imagine your own versions. Just like the storytellers of old, you can help keep these myths alive, ensuring that their magic and wisdom continue to inspire new generations.

The world may have changed since these myths were first told, but the wonder and imagination they inspire are timeless. Wherever your adventures take you next, remember the tales of old—the gods, heroes, and creatures that filled the world with magic and mystery. The journey may end here, but the stories live on, waiting for you to tell them again.

The End.

Milton Keynes UK
Ingram Content Group UK Ltd.
UKHW020758231024
450026UK00001B/98